POLITICS WITHOUT PRINCIPLE : S
DS79.739 .C36 1993

MY 27 '96			
FE 24 '95			
DE 20 '96			
DE 16 '97			
AP 25 '00			
MY 24 '00			
OC 30 '02			
NO 20 '02			
MY 13 '03			

DEMCO 38-296

Politics
Without Principle

*Critical Perspectives
on World Politics*

———— ◇ ————

R. B. J. Walker, Series Editor

Politics Without Principle

Sovereignty, Ethics, and the Narratives of the Gulf War

David Campbell

Lynne Rienner Publishers ◆ Boulder and London

Published in the United States of America in 1993 by
Lynne Rienner Publishers, Inc.
1800 30th Street, Boulder, Colorado 80301

and in the United Kingdom by
Lynne Rienner Publishers, Inc.
3 Henrietta Street, Covent Garden, London WC2E 8LU

Library of Congress Cataloging-in-Publication Data
Campbell, David, 1961-
  Politics without principle : sovereignty, ethics, and the narratives
of the Gulf War / David Campbell.
      p.   cm.
  Includes bibliographical references (p.   ) and index.
  ISBN 1-55587-381-2 (alk. paper)
  1. Persian Gulf War, 1991—Press coverage. 2. Persian Gulf War,
1991—Propaganda. I. Title.
DS79.739.C36   1993
956.704' 42—dc20   92-45229
                                                                CIP

British Cataloguing-in-Publication Data
A Cataloguing-in-Publication record for this book
is available from the British Library.

Printed and bound in the United States of America

The paper used in this publication meets the requirements
of the American National Standard for Permanence of
Paper for Printed Library Materials Z39.48-1984.

Contents

Acknowledgments

A number of people were kind enough to offer comments on and provide critical readings of papers and chapter drafts as this project unfolded. I would like to thank (without burdening them with responsibility) Steven David, Michael Klare, Steve Niva, Diana Ohlbaum, Steve Rosow, Rob Walker, and Daniel Warner. Special thanks are due to James Der Derian, Mick Dillon, Tim Luke, and Kate Manzo for their considerable and generous assistance.

David Campbell

Introduction

This book is an essay that I did not intend to write, but I was inspired, at least in part, by personal concerns.

Following the Iraqi invasion of Kuwait, I, like many others, was absorbed with an eerie and often depressing fascination with the conflict, finding myself on the one hand seemingly in the midst of unfolding events, while on the other devoid of any sense of influence over a social and political drama enveloping all who observed it. Convinced that the war option had been settled upon without a thorough consideration of the alternatives, I found that securing some grounds for criticism in this environment proved to be often futile and always frustrating. In December 1990 and January 1991, I traveled to Australia and Britain, thinking that a certain distance from the center of the allied response would allow, if not encourage, a critical perspective; instead, I was struck by the manner in which those societies were on a war footing at least as jingoistic as that in the United States.

When the air war was two weeks old, I was teaching an undergraduate class on the constitution of state identity in an interdependent world and at the same time was preoccupied with the task of finishing a manuscript linking these themes to U.S. foreign policy. Although I collected as much information as I could on the conflict, trying to piece together those snippets of information critical of official policy that sporadically made their way into the public domain, I had no desire to relive the conflict by writing about it.

Nonetheless, a nagging concern stayed with me. It was that we had just witnessed, as all the triumphant reporting would not let us forget, a war of historic proportions. Yet, life in the United States seemed to proceed quite normally, save for the bountiful display of yellow ribbons, the ever present American flags, and emerging discontent brought on by an economic recession. Then one Saturday, a month or so after the

1

ceasefire ending the war, when reports of Iraqi casualty estimates were beginning to circulate, I was walking home across campus and came upon a crowd of sports fans gathered for pregame festivities. The weather was perfect, a carnival atmosphere was in the air—but I was left with a feeling of unease. How was it possible for the country to have been so connected to and supportive of the prosecution of the war against Iraq, yet to remain so disconnected from and seemingly unconcerned by the deaths of tens if not hundreds of thousands of people in Iraq? Perhaps this situation was facilitated by the leadership's public disavowal of concern over the magnitude of death they had inflicted upon Iraq.[1] Still, this unease highlighted for me what was the most troubling aspect of the war—the apparent equanimity with which so many citizens of "civilized" countries had accepted if not encouraged the death of the Other.[2] Moreover, this equanimity was achieved in the name of a certain morality and a particular principle, for there have been few conflicts in recent times so replete with ethical reasoning as the Gulf War.

The equanimity of the public toward the death of the Other raised for me two fundamental questions: What form of morality and which principles can sanction mass death? And what alternative conception of ethics relevant to foreign policy might reduce the impulse to orgiastic violence? Neither of these questions can be satisfactorily addressed by an essay of this length, but they were the impetus behind my decision to write about the war. To be sure, this essay contains a considerable amount of detail about the conflict and the nature of U.S.-Iraqi-Kuwaiti relations prior to the war. But its major focus is neither those events nor those issues *per se.* Rather, through examination of those events and issues, I seek to address the broader questions of agency, sovereignty, ethics, and responsibility in contemporary global politics, even if this thematic consideration is necessarily preliminary.

I begin this task in Chapter 1 by considering the war in terms of narrative and the authority (author-ity) to narrate, arguing that issues relating to textuality and interpretation, though not entirely novel to this particular war, were crucial to the presentation and representation of the Gulf War to its various publics. By highlighting the figurative nature of the official war story and its subsequent propensity to unravel, I hope to establish the necessary space for a critical consideration of the conflict. In Chapter 2 I focus on the discourse of moral certitude enunciated by the Bush administration in its effort to attribute all responsibility for the crisis to Iraq. There I argue that the administration's effort to present this issue in terms of ethical clarity—guided by the principle of sovereignty—should be understood as part and parcel of the performative constitution of (supposedly) stable identities from within ambiguous and undecidable contexts.

Chapters 3 and 4 demonstrate that, for all the attempts to present the conflict in black and white terms, the events and issues under consideration were in actuality washed in shades of gray. Indeed, it may be precisely because they *were* washed in shades of gray that it was necessary (in terms of the administration's desire to go to war) for them to be narrated as black and white. I try to underscore this by offering counter-narratives of six episodes central to the official war story: the status of the border between Kuwait and Iraq; relations between Iraq, Kuwait, and the United States prior to 2 August 1990; the grievances behind the Iraqi invasion; the diplomatic possibilities for a resolution of the crisis; the way human rights abuses were selectively presented to engender moral outrage; and issues that arose during the prosecution of the war itself. While I do hope to have presented in these chapters some important factors pertaining to the conflict, offering *the* true account that pierces the veil of official propaganda is not my aim.[3] Instead, through these details I hope to offer evidence for my contention that the radically interdependent nature of contemporary world politics renders any attempt to make absolute and emphatic claims about agency, ethics, responsibility, and sovereignty intrinsically problematic.[4] As such, the indefinite, interwoven, and transgressive nature of the events and issues leading up to the Gulf War should be seen as more the norm than the exception for global politics in our time.

In Chapters 5 and 6 I draw some implications from my reading of the events and issues surrounding the war in terms of the broader themes that are my principal concern. I argue that the carnage of the conflict can be seen as evidence of the way the underlying insistences in Western culture (no matter how heterogeneous it may be) toward certainty, order, and stability—what I term the "politics of principle"—encourage violent enactment, for it might be said that it is in war that identity is most effectively (although still contingently) secured.[5] I maintain that this enactment of violent obeisance to order inscribes boundaries such that our complicity in evil is erased, responsibility for evil is assigned to another, and an agent capable of bearing blame is constituted. In these terms, we can argue that war—perhaps more clearly than other political practices—manifests a moral economy of culpability that simultaneously condemns and absolves. Accordingly, war—although said to be simply a response to the infraction of territorial boundaries—is as much if not more concerned with the constitution of ethical borders. Such an understanding might prompt a modification of Clausewitz's famous aphorism (that war is the continuation of politics by other means), allowing us to say that war is the narration of politics/the political by other means.[6] Likewise, this understanding would refigure the belief of a just-war theorist like Michael Walzer (who argued that without borders there is no security), such that we could say that without the project of security and the practices of war there would be no borders to secure.

As a consequence, the actuality of a crisis like the Gulf War forces us to denaturalize the geopolitical discourses and state-centric grammars (themselves undergirded by the metanarrative of subjectivity that has been so central to Western philosophy) through which events in world politics are usually told. Such a move has important implications for rethinking ethics and foreign policy, an effort I tentatively address in Chapter 6. There, informed by the thinking of Emmanuel Levinas, I start to outline what might be involved in a practice of ethical engagement that could disturb and exceed the traditional moral economy of culpability and responsibility manifested in conventional international political practice. Although this should be considered only a first step, the constant articulation of moral absolutism and certitude in U.S. policy throughout the crisis, as well as the propensity toward violence, makes any such effort necessary.

NOTES

1. Leaders of the U.S. military, for example, had gone to considerable lengths to appear at ease with the consequences of their policies. When asked in late March 1991 about the extent of Iraqi casualties, General Colin Powell replied, "It's really not a number I'm terribly interested in." Quoted in Clark, *The Fire This Time,* 42.

2. This concern, along with a shared theoretical commitment, is also evident in James Der Derian's important essay on the war. There he writes:

> A poststructuralist approach closes the distance to death, asking first before any other questions, how is my own identity implicated in a study of the killing of others? This is not to take up an a priori pacifist or belligerent position, but to understand fully the forces in a deterritorialized, hyper-mediated, late modern war already at work to *fix* that position before one has even begun to consider it. (Der Derian, *Antidiplomacy,* 173.)

3. The emphasis of my critique thus distinguishes it from the valuable work of someone like Douglas Kellner. See Kellner, *The Persian Gulf TV War.*

4. This I take to be another distinguishing feature of this analysis. A number of the recent critical accounts of the war simply reverse the attribution of responsibility rather than challenge the poles of the discourse within which responsibility is allocated. As such, instead of wholly blaming Iraq for the crisis, they emphatically denounce the United States as the agent bearing prime responsibility. See, for example, Clark et al., *War Crimes*; and Clark, *The Fire This Time.* Likewise, a number of the critical accounts of Iraqi militarization rely, at least implicitly, on a simple, unified understanding of subjectivity, such that in their effort to point out how "the West" (itself a term that conflates many disparate actors) helped arm Iraq, Iraq is stripped of agency (and responsibility) for the process. See, for example, Timmerman, *The Death Lobby.* Once again, this only reverses the poles of the discourse and puts off a more fundamental reappraisal of the complex nature of agency in contemporary international politics.

5. This identity is, not surprisingly, gendered as masculine. On this theme in relationship to the Gulf War, see Cynthia Enloe, "Making Feminist Sense of the Persian Gulf Crisis," *The Village Voice,* 25 September 1990; and Enloe, "Tie a Yellow Ribbon 'Round the New World Order," *The Village Voice,* 19 February 1991. For a more general discussion of the gendered nature of sovereignty, see Campbell, *Writing Security,* 73–75, 238–239.

6. This thought is prompted by Foucault, "Two Lectures," 90–91, in *Power/Knowledge,* ed. Gordon.

1

War Stories

The event is not what happens.
The event is that which can be narrated.

Telling a story establishes order and meaning. Scripting a narrative, providing a sequentially ordered plot, a cast of characters, identifiable forces, attributable motivations, and lessons for the future, is one of the most common ways we ascribe intelligibility when confronted with the novel or the unfamiliar. As Edith Wyschogrod has observed, "Before the tale comes into being, 'events' are nothing more than a shapeless flux, an anarchic and inchoate nonground."1 Narrativizing is a practice in daily use at multiple sites through numerous actors, but not all participants in the plot share power equally. When it is something as momentous as the United States–led war against Iraq that needs to be comprehended, the narrative functions of our society's privileged storytellers take on added significance. And among those political figures and scholars of international relations to whom narrative authority (author-ity) is granted, one can identify a favored narrative disposition.

Riven with various demands, insistences, and assertions that things "must" be either this or that, this disposition is committed to an epistemic realism, whereby the world comprises material objects whose existence is independent of ideas or beliefs about them; it favors a narrativizing historiography in which things have a self-evident quality that allows them to speak for themselves; and it sanctions a logic of explanation whereby it is the purpose of analysis to identify those self-evident things and material causes so that actors can accommodate themselves to the realm of

7

necessity they engender.[2]

An indebtedness to the narrative disposition of epistemic realism can easily be observed in the official rendering of the war against Iraq. The plot is structured so that it begins with the Iraqi invasion of Kuwait on 2 August 1990 and ends with the ceasefire on 28 February 1991 (although a number of encores occasioned by Kurds, Shiites, and UN Security Council resolutions prolonged it somewhat). The cast involved a multinational assembly of characters—with George Bush in the role of leading man—ranged against the heinous persona of Saddam Hussein, whose erratic lust for power led him to commit a crime that warranted punishment of capital proportions. The drama initially drew such rave reviews that it came to be seen as a triumph for the U.S. production company, a paradigmatic instance of the right way to act, and a shining example worthy of subsequent replication.[3]

In the immediate aftermath of the conflict, this official war story was dominant to such a degree that alternative interpretations were almost totally excluded. With the passage of time and the work of reflection, however, parts of the official account have begun either to unravel or to appear badly tarnished. Questions have been raised about the policy of the United States toward Iraq in the period prior to the conflict, about many aspects of the conduct of the conflict itself, and about the wisdom and integrity of some of the key players in the drama.[4] Yet many of these criticisms—some of which will be considered in more detail in Chapters 3 and 4—are presented as though they comprise the long hidden truth, breaking the ideological power of officialdom and puncturing false consciousness. In other words, many of the challenges to the official war story are equally indebted to epistemic realism, a narrativizing historiography, and a logic of explanation.

It is one of the central purposes of this essay to stress that there is at least one alternative mode of thinking that can avoid the illusions of epistemic realism while offering a political critique relevant to contemporary practice. This mode of thinking, in contrast to epistemic realism, argues that as understanding involves rendering the unfamiliar in terms of the familiar, there is always an ineluctable debt to interpretation such that there is nothing outside of discourse. In contrast to a narrativizing historiography, it employs a mode of historical representation that self-consciously adopts a perspective. And in contrast to the logic of explanation, it embraces a logic of interpretation that acknowledges the improbability of cataloging, calculating, and specifying "real causes," concerning itself instead with considering the manifest political consequences of adopting one mode of representation over another.

Of course, words such as "narrative," "discourse," and "text" often induce anxiety if not apoplexy among those convinced that there exists an unproblematic domain ("the real world") impervious to interpretation. To such true believers, any analytic mode that implicitly or explicitly questions the facticity of the external world is at best misleading and at worst dangerous.[5] It is therefore important to be clear about what is meant by an analysis predicated on the notion that there is nothing outside of discourse. While some practitioners of literary theory in the U.S. academy (though not theorists concerned with international politics) have diminished what Edward Said has termed the "worldliness" of texts, this refusal to overcome fully the discursive/nondiscursive distinction in interpretation is not unavoidable.[6] Ernesto Laclau and Chantal Mouffe have offered an important statement that clarifies this point:

> The fact that every object is constituted as an object of discourse has *nothing to do* with whether there is a world external to thought, or with the realism/idealism opposition. An earthquake or the falling of a brick is an event that certainly exists, in the sense that it occurs here and now, independently of my will. But whether their specificity as objects is constructed in terms of 'natural phenomena' or 'expressions of the wrath of God', depends upon the structuring of a discursive field. What is denied is not that such objects exist externally to thought, but the rather different assertion that they could constitute themselves as objects outside of any discursive condition of emergence.[7]

The impossibility that understanding can occur outside of discourse—which means that the discursive/nondiscursive distinction is unsustainable—is made even more definite in the realm of world politics and international relations by the overtly textual nature of the domain. Indeed, U.S. foreign policy is quite literally concerned with the power of writing and with texts as the facts of power.[8] Following Michel Foucault's observation that what constitutes reality is "the entangled mass of 'documentation' with which a society is always bound up,"[9] we can declare without overstatement that the conduct of foreign policy depends upon and has a predilection for texts. Departmental summaries, National Security Council papers, Presidential Decision documents, memoranda of all kinds, cables from here, there, and everywhere, *aides-memoires, bouts de papier, demarches,* and so on, are the very being of foreign policy and international relations for which "Il n'y a pas de hors-texte."[10] As such, the basis for decisionmaking in foreign policy is invariably some form of mediated experience in which those referents signified as belonging to "external" reality are in actuality "internal" to discourse. It is in this context that Kissinger has argued that "the conjectural element" is at the very heart of policymaking: "the need to gear actions to an assessment that cannot be proved true when it is made."[11]

Nowhere, however, is the role of textual practices in foreign policy clearer than in the production of intelligence assessments. The path from "raw data" to the finished intelligence report is a succession of interpretive practices. The photographic representations, electronic intercepts, and human sources that are employed to collect data all rely on a variety of interpretive codes to make sense of the material with which they are confronted. Even at the stage of "raw data" there is more to the process of understanding than a simple apprehension of experience, because

> the meaning and value imposed on the world is structured not by one's immediate consciousness but by the various reality-making scripts one inherits and acquires from one's surrounding cultural/linguistic condition. The pre-text of apprehension is therefore largely institutionalized and is reflected in the ready-to-hand language practices, the historically produced styles—grammars, rhetorics, and narrative structures—through which the familiar world is continuously interpreted and produced.[12]

These interpretive practices become even more important in the later stages of intelligence production. After the collection of "data," the several tons of paper produced each day by the U.S. intelligence community (largely through the National Security Agency) then has to be sorted and distributed. This processing can involve language translation, deciphering, and various forms of imaging (undertaken by the unambiguously named National Photographic Interpretation Center) before the material is distributed to the various branches of the intelligence community for further interpretation prior to being passed on to various levels of policymakers.[13] Nevertheless, much of the discourse on intelligence in foreign policy analysis begins from the unstated assumption that knowledge is something that can be perfected such that its object of concern can be transparently observed. This assumption is evident in debates that have arisen over the "failure" of intelligence to predict accurately in given cases.[14] What needs to be appreciated is that such debates, even when they posit the existence of external and independent referents, are still functioning within discourse.

The indispensability of interpretation to intelligence and hence to the conduct of foreign policy, as well as questions surrounding the production of knowledge, have become major issues in the aftermath of the Gulf War. Indeed, many if not all of the policy and political disputes that have emerged in the period since the February 1991 ceasefire bear upon the questions of how we come to know, the status of the knowledge that results, and the implications of that knowledge for future action. Debates about the nature of the conflict within the military, concerns about the performance of the Patriot missile and the campaign against Iraq's SCUD launchers, doubts as to whether the United States correctly judged Iraq's intentions prior to August 1990, and assessments of Iraqi troop levels and casualty figures have all involved at their core epistemological questions. While Iraqi troop and casualty numbers will be dealt with in Chapter 4, I want to consider here the first two issues, to underscore the importance of discourse, narrative, and text to policy.

To aid in establishing an official record of the Gulf War so as to guide future decisions, the Pentagon produced a three-volume, 1,300-page report summarizing its view of the conflict.[15] One of its major findings was that the intelligence agencies were not adequately equipped to handle the massive amount of information required for effective conduct of the air campaign against Iraq. The intelligence agencies were unable to assess bomb damage properly and to communicate targeting restrictions speedily to the air forces, such that far greater damage was inflicted upon Iraq's civilian infrastructure than originally intended.[16]

Even more significant, though, as an indication of textuality's importance to the conduct of foreign policy, are the circumstances of the report's genesis. Originally scheduled to be presented on the first anniversary of the conflict, it was delayed while debate internal to the various branches of the armed services raged. As one account noted:

> Divided into eight narrative chapters and 20 appendices, the study was produced by three dozen military drafters under the direction of I. Lewis Libby, the principal deputy undersecretary for policy. It was delayed nearly three months past its Jan. 15 deadline by hundreds of interservice and interagency *disputes over the way the war was fought and the meanings to be extracted from its outcomes.* Most disputes, according to officials involved in the drafting, led to neutral compromise language or the deletion of any mention of the disputed subject.[17]

Thus, although the conflict was hailed as a great triumph by all concerned, when it came down to understanding the nature of the conflict, not even those most closely involved could agree on "the way the war was fought and the meanings to be extracted from its outcomes." Clearly then, even at one of the most fundamental levels of action in foreign policy, it is possible neither to efface the indispensability of interpretation nor to elide the importance of narratives in the scripting of reality. To underscore this point, consider the contention over the performance of the Patriot missile and the air campaign to destroy Iraq's SCUD missiles and their launchers.

The Patriot was originally hailed as almost totally effective against SCUD missiles fired at Israel and Saudi Arabia; the president at one stage during the war declared that the missile, like some able sportsman, was "forty-one for forty-two" in intercepts.[18] It was seen as proof that ballistic missile defenses work; former Pentagon official Richard Perle declared that there could be little debate about this because "the world saw the results."[19] The effectiveness of the Patriot, though, has since been downplayed. Before a congressional hearing in April 1992, army officials who had previously stated publicly that the missile had intercepted forty-five out of forty-seven SCUDs heavily qualified both the numbers involved and the meaning of "intercept." The ratio of success was reduced to 40 percent of the engagements over Israel and 70 percent over Saudi Arabia, and the meaning of "intercept" came to be that "a Patriot and a Scud passed in the sky" rather than one "killed" or "destroyed" the other.[20]

The most interesting aspect of this dispute was that television videotape and the interpretation thereof came to be the evidentiary basis for either side; texts and statements were the arena in which the argument was to be settled. Theodore Postol, who argued in an academic journal that he could find no evidence to support any of the army's claims, relied in large part on the same footage of Patriot/SCUD encounters on the basis of which viewers had previously been led to believe that defeat of the Iraqi missile was nearly total.[21] To counter Postol's argument, Raytheon, the manufacturer of Patriot, mailed a report to subscribers of *International Security* disputing the article,[22] while various proponents of Patriot and ballistic missile defense systems claimed either that Postol had edited the videotape to support his conclusions, or that commercial television cameras operated at a pace too slow to be relied upon to distinguish between hits and misses.[23] Moreover, much of the argument against Postol and other critics was ad hominem or speculative and unrelated to the "facts" at issue. For example, Richard Perle claimed that criticism of the Patriot system was part of the (presumably well-known) "broad opposition on university campuses and a few other places to the notion that the United States should be defended in any serious way."[24] When asked about other problems with the Patriot—such as damage to Israeli urban areas when the Patriot crashed—Perle resorted to futuristic conjecture delivered with declarative authority: "The fact is that future generations of Patriot will intercept at greater distances and the problem won't exist."[25] The campaign against Postol reached its apogee when the army tried, subsequent to publication, to classify his article as secret and began a Defense Investigative Service inquiry into the possible use of military secrets, charges later found to be groundless.[26]

The military experienced more than a few difficulties with film interpretation. Relying upon footage shot from so-called "smart bombs" and attack aircraft as its record of the conflict, and effectively managing public perception of the war as clean and surgical through selective release of videotape at media briefings, the Pentagon sought to objectify representations of engagements in ways that obfuscated their constructed and contested character.[27] Notorious in this regard was the presentation of the air campaign against Iraq's fixed and mobile SCUD launchers. As Mark Crispin Miller has revealed, although the military claimed to have destroyed all the fixed launch sites and over three-quarters of the mobile sites (indeed, when added up, Pentagon briefers had claimed to have destroyed eighty-one SCUD launch sites even though they said Iraq possessed only fifty at the start of the war), the actual numbers turned out to be far smaller.[28] To be precise, *no* mobile launchers were destroyed, very few of the missiles themselves were rendered inoperative, and the meaning of "destroyed" in relation to the fixed sites was debated. Most interestingly, however, it was once again the question of how to interpret video footage that was at the core of the issue. Although one briefer in Riyadh presented film captioned "Mobile SCUD Destruction 28 Jan 91" as "some film that I think will speak for itself," he did so knowing that there had been considerable debate among the staff about whether or not it portrayed what was claimed.[29] Indeed, many suspected that the objects that had been bombed were trucks smuggling fuel from Jordan, a proposition later supported by further intelligence analysis and image enhancement.

Likewise, further analysis of the performance of the Stealth aircraft and of laser-guided weapons such as the Tomahawk cruise missile has produced far lower estimates of success than those previously touted. The success rate claimed was reduced from 90 percent to 60 percent, and "success" was redefined so that a weapon needed only to "disrupt a target's activity" to qualify.[30] Furthermore, as one report stated, "Much of the new analysis is subjective and based on interpretation of photographic evidence of bomb damage."[31] The question as to whether or not the camera can lie has become more complex than ever, for the revised estimates of missile success rates were made necessary by a newly recognized characteristic of the cameras carried on attack aircraft. In the words of one analyst: "One of the problems you have with an infrared TV camera is [that the explosion creates] a blooming effect far greater than the lethal radius of the bomb, so it can look like a direct hit when you've in fact missed."[32]

The dilemma of interpretation revealed in these and other cases was a widespread if not inherently pervasive feature of this conflict. While we think of the military commanders in charge of a campaign as being on "the front line," it is probably more accurate to consider them as only being in "the front row" of a theater, in this case the "Kuwaiti Theater of Operations." Indeed, in an air campaign such as the one that consumed the first six weeks of Desert Storm, there is no single front line and there are no allied observers actually on a front line. Instead, for the pilots, the intelligence analysts, and the commanders (though not for those who live at or near ground zero), it is the hyperspace of video in which they and their

14   POLITICS WITHOUT PRINCIPLE

targets are situated.[33] This environment, which Tom Engelhardt has in-
sightfully described as "total television," effectively completes the dissim-
ulation of any boundaries that may have been posited as distinguishing
the inside from the outside.[34] More conventional renditions of the problem
recognize the issue, even though they persist in placing it within the
traditional register of the objective/subjective conditions of knowledge.
But what is being offered in those formulations as an exceptional problem
should be identified as the normal condition.

For all these reasons, then, characterizing the war against Iraq as a
performance neither diminishes its importance nor trivializes its brutality.
Because the narrative disposition of epistemic realism characterizing most
accounts of the conflict (critical or otherwise) effaces the indispensability
of interpretation, it occludes the manifestly political production of the
dominant narrative. In contrast, the notion of performance highlights the
way in which events and subjects have no ontological status apart from
the countless acts that constitute their reality; it therefore calls attention
to the way in which the supposedly stable, prediscursive grounds appealed
to by categorical judgments, definitive conclusions, and triumphalist narratives are themselves constituted through that appeal.[35] Understanding
the war as a performance, then, can deepen our appreciation of its costs
and consequences by giving us the opportunity to consider alternative
renderings. In short, because the event does not simply exist but has to be
narrated, the notion of performance makes possible the emergence of
disturbing and unsettling aspects of the official narrative of the war with
Iraq.

An analysis of this kind has unmistakable political implications, given
that planning for the next war proceeds according to experience of the last
war. Indeed, the U.S. military, having determined that future threats are
most likely to emerge from the South now that the old threat from the
East has collapsed, is actively laying the groundwork for the next "mid-
dle-level intensity conflict" (MIC), a class of threat that Iraq is said to have
represented.[36] Disturbingly, there is little doubt among senior officials that
there will be another war; former Secretary of Defense Cheney declared
that all future decisions concerning the military budget constituted "preparation for the next time we go to war. There will be a next time. There
always is."[37] And when that next war is upon us, the discursive and political
strategies through which it will be interpreted, narrated, and rationalized
will likely resemble those associated with Desert Shield-cum-Storm.

A number of different analyses of the war with Iraq have already
considered various aspects of the crisis, ranging from detailed assessments
of the U.S. military's performance to mechanical applications of just-war
theory.[38] The purpose of this essay is to take a broader look at the event
narrated by problematizing various episodes in the official story. The

strategy of this argument is to assemble alternative readings around certain crucial elements of the plot, thereby de-naturalizing the celebratory war story painted above. This essay thus serves as a moment of reportage attuned to the theoretical issues surrounding the importance of narrative, discourse, and text discussed above, such that important elements neglected by the dominant narrative are brought together in detail to challenge the comprehensive nature of the war story.

Once upon a time, of course, reportage was the function of the media. Two features of the coverage of the Gulf War, however, militated against proper execution of that function. The first might be termed the failure of will, during the conflict and its build-up, on the part of many media outlets, even those considered the most reputable, and even those that subsequently produced incisive critiques of and damaging revelations about the official war story. Indeed, it is not unfair to suggest that prior to 15 January 1991, none of the renowned newspapers or television shows in the United States adopted a broad, critical perspective that pulled the elements of the crisis together such that its operating assumptions could be examined.[39] The absence of such a perspective was reflected, for example, in the fact that, as the media watchdog FAIR reported, of 878 on-air sources used by the network news broadcasts to consider the conflict, only one was a representative of a national peace organization. Likewise, of the 2,855 minutes of network coverage of the crisis from 8 August 1990 until 3 January 1991, a mere twenty-nine minutes (or 1 percent of airtime) dealt with grassroots dissent, even though opinion polls showed half the country opposed going to war.[40] Perhaps even more insidiously, there were a number of instances in which organizations opposing the war, such as the Military Families Support Network and Physicians for Social Responsibility, were unable to purchase commercial time for announcements stating their position. Refusing airtime to these groups, CNN and network stations in Los Angeles, New York, and Washington claimed the advertisements were "deemed to be unbalanced" and "against policy."[41] At the same time, prowar groups such as Citizens for a Free Kuwait—a lobby organized and managed by the public relations firm, Hill and Knowlton, that was retained by the Kuwaiti government-in-exile—successfully produced and placed advertisements without hindrance, had access to Congress, and even made presentations to the United Nations Security Council.[42]

Despite (though perhaps a contributing factor in) the overwhelming preponderance of media coverage favorable to the administration's position, public opinion polls once the war began showed overwhelming support for media censorship by the military—one poll showed 79 percent of respondents in favor[43]—and offered indications that as many as a quarter of the population favored an outright ban on antiwar demonstrations.[44] In an environment Anna Quindlen described as "high octane Amerimania,"[45] where Arab-Americans found themselves harassed by the FBI, where Pan Am for a while banned Iraqi nationals and those carrying Kuwaiti passports from its flights, where some journalists and local newspaper editors were suspended or fired for expressing antiwar sentiments, and where an Italian basketball player for Seton Hall University was the target of abuse by sports fans because he refused to wear an American flag on his shirt as a symbol of support for the troops,[46] it is perhaps not surprising—although fundamentally disturbing—that some media outlets should have abdicated some responsibility for critical commentary.

To insure that this climate prevailed, a number of political organizations campaigned against any critical coverage that managed to surface. For example, the Republican National Committee distributed preprinted letters to a half-million contributors, calling upon local media outlets to support the troops and criticizing the attention paid to antiwar arguments. Interestingly, this letter was signed by Senator Alan Simpson (R-Wyoming), a man who thought he knew a lot about the media: during a 12 April 1990 Senate delegation meeting with President Hussein in Baghdad, he had opined that the Iraqi leader's only problem in the West was the "haughty and pampered" media, while a few months later during the war with Iraq he branded CNN correspondent Peter Arnett a "sympathizer" for reporting from Baghdad.[47]

The second and probably more significant feature of the conflict that militated against critical commentary was the speed of the conflict, its videographic nature, and the environment of total television in which it was conducted. Aside from the structural impediments of the pool system of media coverage (in which only 192 out of the 1,400 journalists in Saudi Arabia were placed, and because of which journalists could be more easily indirectly censored and manipulated by the military),[48] the fact that "the war's juggernaut pace 'outstripped the established system for collecting and reporting intelligence'" meant that it also outstripped the established modes of journalistic analysis regardless of critical intent.[49] Moreover, just as the military found itself located in video hyperspace for the conduct of the war, the media found itself a coproducer of this virtual reality, ineluctably drawn into the constitution of the object it purported to stand apart from and observe critically.[50]

This situation poses a truly immense challenge to the task of preserving a democratic culture in which a multitude of vantage points can be aired for contestation and debate. If, even when they can resist the pressures and temptations of the cultural and political orthodoxy, the media find themselves implicated in the processes they wish to subject to scrutiny, we can no longer comfort ourselves with the thought that there inevitably exists an untainted source of commentary and critique. This essay is without doubt an inadequate response to this challenge, but insofar as it seeks to foreground the narrative practices implicated in the constitution of our knowledge of the Gulf War, and thus to highlight the issues and possibilities excluded, it offers one strategy for avoiding automatic submission to officially scripted accounts. To this end, I want to examine the political discourse of moral certitude that mobilized the coalition led by the United States and the extent to which prewar policies, the conduct of the war, and postwar legacies justify this figuration of the conflict.

In the five-month period between the Iraqi invasion of Kuwait and the beginning of the war to reverse it, the contours of the policy debate—in a haunting echo of Britain's 1982 decision to recapture the Falkland/Malvinas Islands from Argentina—approximated neither the rational ideal of crisis management nor the conspiracy theory of unfettered war mongering.[51] Instead, this was a period marked by deep apprehension and manifold contradictions, which gave rise to a social and political drama enacted so as to enable both the players and the audience to make the transition from peace to war. As a rite of passage, this drama constituted a new reality in which history could be suspended, in order that certain fears be assuaged, doubts expunged, and tensions resolved.[52] Pivotal to the drama was the discourse of moral certitude.

NOTES

The epigraph that opens this chapter is quoted from Feldman, *Formations of Violence*, 14.

1. Wyschogrod, *Saints and Postmodernism*, 6–7.

2. See White, *The Content of the Form*, especially Chapter 1; and Bruner, "The Narrative Construction of Reality." For a discussion of these entailments in international relations, see Campbell, "Recent Changes in Social Theory"; and George, "International Relations and the Search for Thinking Space." It needs to be emphasized that "epistemic realism" is a metatheoretical disposition the entailments of which are evident in theoretical positions (such as political realism and liberalism) distinguished within the discipline of international relations. On the relationship of epistemic realism and political realism, see Connolly, "Democracy and Territoriality," 483n.

3. Should this appear rather melodramatic, consider the rendering of the war offered on its first anniversary by a senior congressional Democrat, to ward off the interpretations of "revisionists" and "naysayers": see Stephen Solarz, "A Worthy War," *New York Times*, 19 January 1992, E19.

4. For an overview, see "Bush's Greatest Glory Fades As Questions on Iraq Persist," *New York Times*, 27 June 1992, 1. For a rejoinder that rejects many of the criticisms, see Shibley Telhami, "Did We Appease Iraq?" *New York Times*, 29 June 1992, 15.

5. For one of the many observations in international relations literature that exhibit this prejudice, see Walt, "The Renaissance of Security Studies," 223.

6. Said, *The World, the Text, and the Critic,* 4.

7. Laclau and Mouffe, *Hegemony and Socialist Strategy,* 108.

8. "As Nietzsche had the perspicacity to see, texts are fundamentally facts of power, not of democratic exchange." Said, *The World, the Text, and the Critic,* 45.

9. Rajchman, *Michel Foucault,* 51.

10. This, of course, is Derrida's (in)famous and more often than not misunderstood declaration. See Derrida, *Of Grammatology,* 158. For an amplification of this theme, see Derrida, "But, beyond . . .," especially 167–168; and Carroll, *Paraesthetics,* especially 96–97. Combining the insights of Derrida and Foucault in this context should not be taken as suggesting they were in total agreement on these issues. To the contrary, there was an active tension if not "polemical conflict" between these two thinkers on the question of textuality. See Said, *The World, the Text, and the Critic,* 183–192.

11. Quoted in Shafer, *Deadly Paradigms,* 31. For discussions of the textuality of defense policymaking, see Dillon, *Defense, Discourse and Policy Making.*

12. Michael Shapiro, "Textualizing Global Politics," in *International/Intertextual Relations,* ed. Der Derian and Shapiro, 11.

13. For a description of these processes and the product that emerges from them, see Richelson, *The U.S. Intelligence Community,* Chapter 12.

14. See, for example, "U.S. Intelligence Was Faulty on Iraq," *Washington Post,* 9 May 1992, A10.

15. U.S. Department of Defense, *Conduct of the Persian Gulf War.*

16. "Pentagon Study Cites Problems With Gulf Efforts," *New York Times,* 23 February 1992, A1; and "Pentagon Report on Persian Gulf War: A Few Surprises and Some Silences," *New York Times,* 11 April 1992, 4. While there seems little doubt that the military has been forthcoming about problems in intelligence and information processing during the conflict, the conclusion that these problems were responsible for the massive damage inflicted upon Iraq's civilian infrastructure seems a little disingenuous. Although we cannot rule out that intelligence difficulties did result in increased levels of "collateral damage," there can likewise be little doubt that much of this damage was intentionally inflicted. Most particularly, the fact that 215 combat sorties were flown against twenty-five electrical installations cannot be explained away by problems with information.

17. "Gulf War Failures Cited," *Washington Post,* 11 April 1992, A1 and A12. Emphasis added.

18. "Patriot Games," *New York Times,* 9 April 1992, A24.

19. *Nightline,* 6 April 1992.

20. "Army Cuts Claims of Patriot Success," *Washington Post,* 8 April 1992, A1 and A8.

21. Postol, "Lessons of the Gulf War Experience with Patriot."

22. A version of this can be found in Stein and Postol, "Correspondence."

23. "Critic of Patriot Missile Says It Was 'Almost Total Failure' in War," *New York Times,* 9 January 1992; *Nightline,* 6 April 1992; and "Army Cuts Claims of Patriot Success," *Washington Post,* 8 April 1992.

24. Quoted on *Nightline,* 6 April 1992.

25. Quoted on *Nightline,* 6 April 1992.

26. Stein and Postol, "Correspondence," 239–240n.

27. Most obviously, the Pentagon achieved this in the year following the end of the war by continuing to refuse to publicly screen their video footage of weapons

missing their target. "Gulf Weapons' Accuracy Downgraded," *Washington Post,* 10 April 1992, A1.

28. Mark Crispin Miller, "Operation Desert Sham," *New York Times,* 24 June 1992, A21. See also "Pentagon Claims on SCUDs Disputed," *New York Times,* 24 June 1992, A6.

29. Quoted in Miller, "Operation Desert Sham."

30. "Gulf Weapons' Accuracy Downgraded," *Washington Post,* 10 April 1992. Quote at A8.

31. "Gulf Weapons' Accuracy Downgraded," *Washington Post,* 10 April 1992.

32. "Gulf Weapons' Accuracy Downgraded," *Washington Post,* 10 April 1992.

33. Der Derian, "Videographic War II."

34. Tom Engelhardt, "The Gulf War as Total Television," *The Nation,* 11 May 1992.

35. Campbell, *Writing Security,* especially the introduction. Moreover, many aspects of the war with Iraq, most notably the military briefings given by allied officials, had an explicitly performative quality. For an analysis, see Robert Fisk, "Bloodless Theatre of War at the Riyadh Hyatt Hotel," *The Independent* (London), 13 February 1991, 1.

36. See "Pentagon Imagines New Enemies to Fight in Post–Cold War Era," *New York Times,* 17 February 1991, A1. On the place of MIC scenarios in Pentagon thinking, see Michael Klare, "The Pentagon's New Paradigm," in *The Gulf War Reader,* ed. Sifry and Cerf; Klare, "Policing the Gulf—And the World," *The Nation,* 15 October 1990; and Klare, "One, Two, Many Iraqs," *The Progressive,* April 1991.

37. Senate Armed Services Committee, *Hearing on FY 93 Defense Budget.*

38. For strategic reviews, see Friedman, *Desert Victory;* Freedman and Karsh, "How Kuwait Was Won"; and Halliday, "The Gulf War and its Aftermath." On just war, see Johnson and Weigel, eds., *Just War and the Gulf War.*

39. James Bennet, "How the Media Missed the Story," in *The Gulf War Reader,* ed. Sifry and Cerf. Other critical analyses of the media's role can be found in Boot, "Operation Deep Think"; "Free to Report What We Are Told," *The Independent,* 6 February 1991, 19; Alexander Cockburn, "The Press and the 'Just War'," *The Nation,* 18 February 1991; and Sydney H. Schanberg, "A Muzzle for the Press," in *The Gulf War Reader.* See also Grace Paley, "Something About the Peace Movement: Something About the People's Right *Not* to Know," in *The Gulf Between Us,* ed. Brittain; Tiffen, "Marching to Whose Drum?" and Gottschalk, "Operation Desert Cloud." Recent book-length treatments of this issue include Kellner, *The Persian Gulf TV War;* and Taylor, *War and the Media.* Having failed to exercise their analytical functions before and during the war, a number of major media outlets sought implicitly to exonerate themselves after the war by criticizing the strictures of military censorship they had previously accepted. "15 Top Journalists See Cheney and Object to Gulf War Curbs," *New York Times,* 2 May 1991, A16; and "17 News Executives Criticize U.S. For 'Censorship' of Gulf Coverage," *New York Times,* 3 July 1991, A4.

40. Cited in Geyer and Green, *Lines in the Sand,* 144.

41. Yant, *Desert Mirage,* 46; and Arthur E. Rowse, "Flacking for the Emir," *The Progressive,* May 1991, 21.

42. Yant, *Desert Mirage;* Rowse, "Flacking for the Emir."

43. Fialka, *Hotel Warriors,* 62.

44. LaMarche, "Managed News, Stifled Views," 70.

45. Anna Quindlen, "Reservations Not Accepted," *New York Times,* 24

February 1991, E17.

46. LaMarche, "Managed News, Stifled Views."

47. Transcript of Meeting Between U.S. Senators and Saddam Hussein, in *The March to War,* Ridgeway, ed., 37; and Yant, *Desert Mirage,* 50–51.

48. LaMarche, "Managed News, Stifled Views," 55–57. See also Fialka, *Hotel Warriors.*

49. "Gulf War Failures Cited," *Washington Post,* 11 April 1992, A12. This was exacerbated by the pool system, which meant in some cases that the transmission times for stories and photos from the battlefield exceeded the twenty-four hours it took stories of the Battle of Bull Run to reach New York during the Civil War. Fialka, *Hotel Warriors,* 2.

50: Engelhardt, "The Gulf War as Total Television."

51. Dillon, *The Falklands, Politics and War,* especially Chapter 5.

52. Dillon, *The Falklands, Politics, and War,* particularly 101–104.

2

Black and White

Truth on this side of the Pyrenees, error beyond . . .

There have been few if any conflicts in recent times so starkly portrayed as the Gulf War. Debates concerning Iraq's invasion of Kuwait reverberated with postulates of ethical reasoning and declarations of moral absolutes.[1] In a prewar interview with David Frost, U.S. President Bush steadfastly asserted that the crisis in the Persian Gulf was "a clear case of . . . good versus evil. We have such a clear moral case. . . . It's that big. It's that important. Nothing like this since World War II. Nothing of this moral importance since World War II."[2] In postwar speeches, Bush maintained that the war was an instance of "selflessly confronting evil for the sake of good in a land so far away," and declared that the United States "went halfway around the world to do what is moral and just and right."[3] Statements of this kind are often dismissed as rhetorical puffery, but there seems little doubt that Bush, as one of his staffers commented, was "a man obsessed and possessed by his mission" of reversing the Iraqi invasion.[4] Combined with the often repeated comparison of Iraqi President Hussein to Hitler, these discursive strategies reproduced the script of World War II—the last unambiguously "good war" in U.S. memory, with its clearly identifiable protagonists and unquestionably noble cause—and worked to erase the memory of Vietnam.[5]

The administration was so preoccupied with "kicking the Vietnam syndrome" that it often seemed caught in a time warp and disengaged from the "reality" of Iraq; Vietnam was the determinative negative reflection, representing all the things that conflict with Iraq would not be, at the same

21

time as it served as the guide to what should be. Learning from experience may be a virtue, but in this case the parameters of that experience were severely circumscribed, for in the terms of official discourse the malady that Vietnam signified was the failure of defeat rather than the folly of intervention.[6] For all the attempt to draw a contrast between the two experiences of conflict, however, many of the features of the war in Vietnam resonated with the campaign against Iraq. Most notable in this regard was the reproduction of the myth of the frontier, in which territorial space becomes intertwined with ethical identity such that the fluid boundary and persistent struggle between "civilization" and "barbarism" is rendered in terms of geopolitical conflict.[7] Just as enemy territory in Vietnam was referred to as "Indian territory," so too was the same said of Iraq.[8] And just as the United States had, under the guise of civilized behavior, perpetrated unspeakable acts against Indians and Vietnamese—acts that included the mutilation of victims' bodies as spoils of war—so too has it been alleged that U.S. servicemen in the Gulf collected the severed limbs of Iraqi soldiers as trophies.[9] The Gulf conflict and the discourse of moral certitude that ratified it can thus be seen as another instance of the orientalist and long-held disposition in the United States to seek regeneration of the self through violence.[10] In this context, George Bush's postwar reflection that "America rediscovered itself during Desert Storm" takes on additional significance.[11] Indeed, this understanding of the conflict seemed to satisfy a widely felt desire. As the *New York Times* concluded in a postwar assessment:

> Since the demise of the Soviet "Evil Empire" there has been a hunger among Americans for a moral clarity to justify and shape their foreign policy, and Mr. Hussein provided it in spades. The physical clarity inherent in military action . . . and the moral clarity provided by Mr. Hussein have made this a surprisingly popular war.[12]

At the basis of this moral certitude and central to the justification of the United States–led military response was the invocation of a principle. "No one . . . wants war," President Bush declared, "but there are times when a country, when all countries who value the principles of sovereignty and independence, must stand against aggression."[13] Iraq's crime, the commander-in-chief argued, was that its "leaders are trying to wipe an internationally recognized sovereign state, a member of the Arab League and the United Nations, off the face of the map."[14] While Bush acknowledged that "there is much in the modern world that is subject to doubts or question—washed in shades of gray," there was no room for doubt about "the brutal aggression of Saddam Hussein. . . . It's black and white. The facts are clear. The choice unambiguous. Right vs. wrong."[15]

The intersection of the politics of principle and the claims of moral righteousness in the discourse of the Gulf War was neither accidental nor fortuitous. Although any number of explanations or rationalizations of U.S. policy were advanced during the deliberations prior to the conflict, it was upon the conviction that this was a just cause that most arguments came to rest.[16] Whether or not the proponents of armed conflict with Iraq explicitly invoked just-war theory, it is in that body of theory where any violation of the principle of sovereignty constitutes the primary trigger for a just conflict.[17]

Indeed, in Michael Walzer's extended discussion of just-war theory, territorial integrity and political sovereignty are the absolute rights of nations in a world comprised of independent states. Their violation constitutes aggression, "a singular and undifferentiated crime because, in all its forms, it challenges rights [territorial integrity and political sovereignty] that are worth dying for."[18] This understanding places a premium on borders. It grants a "presumptive value to the boundaries that mark off a people's territory and to the state that defends it," because borders are the lines that establish a shared space for the exercise of our common life. As Walzer argues:

> The boundaries that exist at any moment in time are likely to be arbitrary, poorly drawn, the products of ancient wars. The mapmakers are likely to have been ignorant, drunken, or corrupt. Nevertheless, these lines establish a habitable world. Within that world, men and women (let us assume) are safe from attack; once the lines are crossed, safety is gone. I don't want to suggest that every boundary dispute is a reason for war. Sometimes adjustments should be accepted and territories shaped so far as possible to the actual need of nations. Good borders make good neighbors. But once an invasion has begun, it may be necessary to defend a bad border simply because there is no other. . . . It is only common sense, then, to attach great importance to boundaries. Rights in the world have value only if they also have dimension.[19]

Walzer recognizes that not every independent state is free, and that certain circumstances can compromise an absolute ban on boundary crossings. Nonetheless, he reasserts his belief that

> the recognition of sovereignty is the only way we have of establishing an arena within which freedom can be fought for and (sometimes) won. It is this arena and the activities that go on within it that we want to protect, and we protect them, much as we protect individual integrity, by marking out boundaries that cannot be crossed, rights that cannot be violated.[20]

It was this argument that led Walzer to declare on the eve of the war, in support of his judgment that the approaching conflict was a just war, "There is no security without borders."[21]

It seems, therefore, that the moral indignation surrounding the conflict in the Gulf was driven solely by the interpretation of Iraq's territorial aggression; according to this interpretation, Iraq, having violated a putatively secure international norm, was the worthy object of enmity and scorn. As critics frequently protested, however, during the Gulf crisis, there have been numerous other violations of the norm of sovereignty in recent years, none of which have given rise to either the magnitude or intensity of opposition that confronted Iraq. Were borders truly invested with the value Walzer ascribes to them, international political practice in recent times might have followed a different course, one in which the sovereignty of East Timor, Lebanon, or Panama, for example, might have been more stoutly defended by the same international community that was outraged by Iraq.

Moreover, had the presumptive value of borders been so self-evident that aggression assumed the outlines of the singular and undifferentiated crime detailed by Walzer, the extensive discourse of moral certitude enacted by the Bush administration would have been superfluous. One does not need to insist unrelentingly that one's cause is just if there is no doubt about the nature of the infraction it seeks to reverse. Therefore, to see the issue solely in a spatial frame, as one of lines in the sand—whether they be crossed by Saddam Hussein or drawn by George Bush—denudes this crisis of political content. The emphasis in both the Gulf War and just-war theory upon borders and their transgression does, however, open the way for a critical consideration of the conflict.

States are paradoxical entities. Devoid of prediscursive and stable identities, they have to be enacted through a variety of political practices (such as foreign policy) that operate in their name while effacing their dependence upon representation. Such practices seek to establish an alignment between territoriality and the various dimensions of identity, so that it becomes possible to speak of a particular state with a definable character. Yet, because identity has meaning only through its relationship with difference, the processes of inscription through which a political community is imagined involve numerous disciplinary practices working to contain contingency and to distance the "self" from the "other." Boundaries are thereby constructed, spaces demarcated, standards of legitimacy incorporated, interpretations of history privileged, alternatives marginalized, and "secure" identities established. In this context, the idea of a border takes on added dimensions and different resonances, such that we can suggest a distinction between the *territorial boundaries of the state* and the *ethical borders of identity*.[22] This is a heuristic distinction only, for it is not possible to disengage geographical partitions from the moral spaces to which they give rise. Nevertheless, this distinction serves as a means by which to unpack the manifestly political nature of the production of state identity.

Distinguishing the ethical borders from the territorial boundaries of state identity also refigures the way in which we understand sovereignty. Instead of regarding sovereignty as simply a legal principle capable of being represented on a map, by focusing upon the various dimensions conflated within the idea of a border, we disclose the way in which sovereignty involves relations of power that establish authority, hierarchy, and criteria for judgment.[23] Nowhere is this more evident than in just-war theory's condition that in order to interpret an act as aggression and the resulting conflict as just, "right authority" must be exercised by a duly constituted sovereign power.[24] What this requires is that a state—the only political authority recognized by just-war theory—or a state-substitute (such as the United Nations) be the body that reaches the decision regarding the need to employ force. Therefore, it is always the state(s) going to war that will determine whether or not war is necessary and just.

This feature of just-war theory is most obvious in Walzer's notion of the "supreme emergency" (which contains more than a slight echo of Carl Schmitt's declaration, "Sovereign is he who decides on the exception").[25] In Walzer's "supreme emergency," a state that believes it is threatened, even if an act of aggression has not been committed, can take actions that might in other circumstances be considered unjust.[26] As such, the identification of aggression and the ascription of "justness" are not achieved by appealing to a neutral foundation or nonpartisan judge; they are achieved through a relation of power that constructs a hierarchy of superior/inferior, in which states associating themselves with the former can punish ones they represent in terms of the latter. Moreover, it means that just-war theory—rather than providing the critique of realism that many proponents claim it does—bears a striking affinity to the logic of raison d'état.[27]

The discourse of moral certitude in the Gulf crisis was thus more than rhetorical icing upon an empirical cake. While no one doubts that the Iraqi invasion of Kuwait was a territorial transgression (although, as shall be argued below, the status of the border crossed was contested), the constitution of that transgression as a crime demanding a full-scale response required a number of interpretive acts. Of course, constituting an act as aggression always requires interpretation. While the United Nations worked strenuously in the 1970s to write an all-encompassing definition of aggression grounded in the use of armed force by one state against another, the charter adopted explicitly invests the Security Council with interpretive latitude. The second of eight articles in the agreement notes that while the use of armed force is prima facie evidence of aggression, the Security Council can decide that a determination of aggression would not be justified in "the light of other relevant circumstances." Similarly, the eighth article of the agreement gives the Security Council authority to name acts other than armed force as aggression.[28] Thus, the claims of right vs. wrong and good vs. evil, enunciated in the discourse of moral certitude, were indispensable to and intertwined with this process of interpretation and worked to constitute the crime that they purportedly only described, thereby inscribing the ethical borders of identity in such a way that the violation of a territorial boundary was an outrage.

Likewise, distinguishing between ethical borders and territorial boundaries in the Gulf crisis allows us to appreciate how the Bush administration's discourse of moral certitude served to instantiate an identity for "America" and "the West" through its rendering of Iraq. To be sure, there have been few regimes in the world less attractive than Baathist Iraq. Nevertheless, even an object of enmity such as Iraq comes to have meaning only through an interpretive process that satisfies the entailments of identity of those figuring Iraq as repugnant. Because a notion of who/what "we" are is intertwined with an understanding of who/what "we" are not and who/what "we" fear, "Iraq" exists in a discursive economy out of which the "United States" (among others) draws and accumulates the moral capital necessary to secure its identity.[29]

The figuration of American identity that results from a discursive economy of this kind is, perhaps more so than that of other states, notoriously amorphous and unstable.[30] As George Bush declared to Congress during Operation Desert Storm: "Halfway around the world, we are engaged in a great struggle in the skies and on the seas and sands. We know why we're there. We are Americans—part of something larger than ourselves."[31] In this and other speeches, administration spokespersons defined their purpose by talking in dichotomous terms reminiscent of the recently ended Cold War: "freedom" versus "tyranny," the "rule of law" versus "lawless aggression," "decency" versus "barbarism," etc. Likewise, media reports juxtaposed the "allied military" with the Iraqi "war machine," our "boys" versus their "hordes," and the "assured" George Bush in contrast to the "crackpot monster" Saddam Hussein.[32] Accordingly, the social space of inside/outside intrinsic to the American (or Western) state both was made possible by and helped constitute a deterritorialized moral space of superior/inferior, which could be animated in terms of any number of figurations of higher/lower. That which distinguished the just and righteous American (or Western) "self" from the evil and abominable Iraqi "other" thus constituted the transgression of the territorial border as a crime and inscribed for the protagonists the ethical borders of their state identity.[33]

The performative constitution of stable identities from within undecidable contexts has as one of its main effects the location of responsibility in a readily identifiable agent. It is hard to imagine modern life without responsibility, but given the many efforts to suppress contingency, it is equally difficult to remember that "life exceeds, resists, and overflows the mold of responsibility imposed upon it."[34] While this recognition invites us to think of responsibility as an ambiguous practice sensitive to the interdependencies of identity, the modern commitment to a settled and unified self (no matter how fragile) spurs investment of responsibility for evil in the other:

> The basic idea behind this formation is that for every evil there must be a responsible agent who deserves to be punished and that for every quotient of evil in the world there must be a corollary quotient of assignable responsibility. No evil without responsibility. No responsibility without reward or punishment according to desert.[35]

In the domain of international relations, these tensions are magnified by the operation of politics on a global scale. Tracing the contours of agency and working to install responsibility within transnational parameters together exacerbate the tendencies toward resentment and otherness already sequestered within sovereign formations. Pursuing simplicity out of complexity and certitude out of ambiguity compels the unrelenting inscription of borders. Foreign policy can consequently be understood as an ethical power of segregation, the purpose of which is to constitute agency in the form of the state and to assign responsibility through the inscription of a geography of evil.[36]

Yet, for all the power located within borders as putatively fixed as those that guided the United States and its allies through the rites of passage in the Gulf crisis, these frontiers remain contingent and contestable. Contrary to President Bush's assurance that war with Iraq was one of those rare events not "washed in shades of gray," many aspects of the conduct of the conflict transgress the appearance of settled and undisputed boundaries between "us" and "them." Indeed, it is precisely because so many of the features of the crisis could not be rendered easily in shades of black and white that the claim about the conflict's unequivocally moral status had to be so insistently made. Moreover, when one examines closely the contours of agency in many of the crisis's episodes, what is revealed is a tangled network of relationships—private/public, overt/covert, corporate/national, economic/military, and combinations of each—that muddies more than a little any attempt to locate the responsibility for evil in one agent rather than another.

The complexity of these networks and relationships, particularly given the dominance of a narrative that has occluded so much, requires a detailed analysis of a number of issues and events. Accordingly, the next two chapters outline alternative readings of six elements elided by the celebratory narrative of war with Iraq: Chapter 3 deals with the status of the border between Iraq and Kuwait, with relations among Iraq, the United States, and other Western countries in the period prior to 2 August

1990, and with the grievances behind the Iraqi invasion; while Chapter 4 discusses the diplomatic possibilities for a non-military resolution to the crisis after 2 August 1990, the role of human rights abuses in locating the responsibility for evil with Iraq, and the conduct of the war that began on 16 January 1991. Each of these counternarratives contributes to a consideration of the questions of agency, responsibility, and sovereignty.

NOTES

The epigraph that opens this chapter is from Pascal, quoted in Schurmann, *Heidegger on Being and Acting,* 294.

1. See "Bush and Saddam's Holy War of Words," *Washington Post,* 3 February 1991, A22; and "Bush Casts Saddam as the Villain in a Fiercely Personal Test of Wills," *Washington Post,* 23 February 1991, A17. There were, of course, many instances of moral posturing on the part of the Iraqis—for example, President Hussein's radio broadcast of 17 January 1991: "The great showdown in the Mother of Battles has started, between victorious truth and defeated error." Quoted in Simpson, *From the House of War,* 314.

2. Quoted in Woodward, *The Commanders,* 343.

3. Quoted in Luke, "The Discipline of Security Studies and the Codes of Containment," 335, 336.

4. "Describing Moral Debate, Bush Spellbinds Audience," *Washington Post,* 26 January 1991, A1. For a testimony to Bush's intense and privately expressed moral commitments, see Rowland Evans and Robert Novak, "St. George and His Dragon," *Washington Post,* 17 December 1990, A11; and Schwarzkopf, *It Doesn't Take a Hero,* 378.

5. Luke, "The Discipline of Security Studies and the Codes of Containment," 333–340.

6. Young, "This is Not Vietnam, This is Not a Pipe"; and Tucker and Hendrickson, *The Imperial Temptation,* Chapter 13.

7. Campbell, *Writing Security,* 164–166. One reviewer has made the interesting observation, consistent with this point, that some of the recent journalistic accounts of how the war was covered replicate captivity narratives. Stephen Hubbell, "Iraq Around the Clock," *The Nation,* 23 March 1992.

8. For details on how the Indian metaphor played out in Vietnam, see Drinnon, *Facing West,* especially Chapter 30.

9. David Corn, "Beltway Bandits," *The Nation,* 4 May 1992.

10. See Slotkin, *Regeneration Through Violence.*

11. Quoted in "Glittering TV Show Dulls Democrats' View of '92," *New York Times,* 5 April 1991, B6.

12. "The Uncertain Time Beyond High Noon," *New York Times,* 24 February 1991, E1.

13. "Address to the People of Iraq on the Persian Gulf Crisis, 16 September 1990," *Weekly Compilation,* 1390.

14. "Remarks Following Discussions With Amir Jabir al-Ahmad al-Jabir Al-Sabah of Kuwait, 29 September 1990," *Weekly Compilation,* 1476.

15. Quoted in Yant, *Desert Mirage,* 54.

16. For a review of the failure of other rationalizations of policy, see

"Selling Sacrifice: Gulf Rationale Still Eludes Bush," *New York Times,* 16 November 1990, A12.

17. On a number of occasions, most notably in a speech to the National Religious Broadcasters Convention on 28 January 1991, President Bush explicitly invoked elements of just-war theory. See Geyer and Green, *Lines in the Sand,* 27, 30, 88, 114, 128, 136–137, 147. For extended discussions of the issue, see Johnson and Weigel, eds., *Just War and the Gulf War;* Brugger, "Was the Gulf War 'Just'?" Cloyd and Elshtain, eds., *The Gulf War and Just War;* and Decosse, ed., *But Was It Just?* Of course, not every legitimate authority concurred in the ascription of "justness" to the war: Pope John Paul II, for one, opposed the conflict. In an address on 12 January 1991, the Pope declared that war would be a "tragic adventure," which would mark "the decline of the whole of humanity." *Facts on File,* 17 January 1991, 30. After the war, an editorial in a Vatican paper, thought to represent often the official view of the Holy See, argued the inadequacy of just-war theory in an era of total war. La Civilta Cattolica, "Modern War and the Christian Conscience," trans. Peter Heinegg, in *But Was it Just?* ed. Decosse.

18. Walzer, *Just and Unjust War,* 53.

19. Walzer, *Just and Unjust War,* 57–58.

20. Walzer, *Just and Unjust War,* 89. For his exceptions to the rule of sovereignty, see 90–91. Walzer's strategy of argumentation here has been called "tantalizingly equivocal" by one critic. Holmes, *On War and Morality,* 170.

21. Walzer, "On Just Wars," 41.

22. Campbell, *Writing Security,* Introduction, Chapter 4.

23. Campbell, *Writing Security,* Chapter 3.

24. James Turner Johnson, "The Just War Tradition and the American Military," in *Just War and the Gulf War,* ed. Johnson and Weigel, 23–24.

25. Schmitt, *Political Theology,* 5.

26. See Walzer, *Just and Unjust Wars,* Chapter 16.

27. Holmes, *On War and Morality,* 167–173. Indeed, there have been a number of critiques of Walzer's position on the grounds that his theory of aggression grants moral status to immoral states and leaves individuals in the lurch. See Doppelt, "Walzer's Theory of Morality in International Relations"; and Luban, "Just War and Human Rights." Walzer's reply is to be found in Walzer, "The Moral Standing of States." The debate continued with Doppelt, "Statism Without Foundations"; and Luban, "The Romance of the Nation-State."

28. Holmes, *On War and Morality,* 162–163.

29. Przybylowicz and JanMohmed, "The Economy of Moral Capital in the Gulf War."

30. See Campbell, *Writing Security,* especially Chapters 5 and 6. The outcome of the Gulf War produced some revealing declarations of "American-ness." Consider the statement of golfer Paul Azinger: "Pride in the United States is back. We went over and thumped the Iraqis and now we've won the Ryder Cup. I'm proud to be American." Quoted in "World of Broken Dreams," *The Independent,* 24 December 1991, 22.

31. "Text of President Bush's State of the Union Message to Nation," *New York Times,* 30 January 1991, A12.

32. All these contrasts, and many others, were used in one week of press coverage by the British press. See "Mad Dogs and Englishmen," in *Despatches from the Gulf,* ed. MacArthur, 123–125.

33. For examples of how the discourse in Germany and the United States functioned in these terms, see Link, "Fanatics, Fundamentalists, Lunatics, and

Drug Traffickers"; and Schulte-Sasse and Schulte-Sasse, "War, Otherness, and Illusionary Identifications with the State."

34. Connolly, *Identity/Difference*, 115.
35. Connolly, *Identity/Difference*, 78.
36. Campbell, *Writing Security*, Chapter 4.

3

Washed in Shades of Gray I

I don't ever want to kill anybody again. . . . The country didn't get to see the cost of the war. I did. They didn't see Iraqi mothers get killed. . . . All in all, I didn't feel they were the bloodthirsty, amoral people we had heard they were.

The ambivalence of Lieutenant Jeffrey N. Zaun, who made the above comments, is a leitmotif for the way that many of the central themes articulated by the United States and its allies in support of the war with Iraq exhibit greater ambiguity when subjected to further examination. Zaun was a national figure as one of the coalition prisoners of war shown on Iraqi television during the conflict, but the story containing his postwar reflections was buried among reports of the New York ticker tape parade held to welcome home the troops. Nor was he alone in his views, for at least five British officers resigned their commissions after seeing the effects of cluster bombs and fuel-air explosives on Iraqi soldiers.[1]

My purpose in Chapters 3 and 4 of this volume is to detail the complexity of the issues the United States and its allies rendered as unambiguous in their official discourse. In their own way, each of the episodes highlighted in these chapters manifests themes important to the overall argument, such as the intricate interrelationships that comprise agency, the problems associated with the definitive location of responsibility with one actor over another, the inherent textuality of international issues such as these, and the difficulty in drawing precise distinctions between the civilian and military realms. Although the recounting of these alternative stories brings together information previously dispersed, I do not claim to break new ground here. Because of the power of the official war story, however, a considerable and detailed effort is required so as to pry open the space for an alternative interpretation of the conflict.

LINES IN THE SAND

Perhaps no single element of the dominant war story is more surprising than the revelation that the territorial boundary between Iraq and Kuwait was as conditional as the ethical border. Given all the protestations about the principle of sovereignty as the fundamental norm transgressed by Iraq on 2 August 1990, the one factor in the Gulf crisis expected to be least susceptible to contestation is the status of the international boundary separating the two countries. Yet, when George Bush came to draw his line in the sand, his maps may have been of little assistance in locating it.

The United States has in actuality never recognized a legally binding border separating Iraq and Kuwait, because no officially ratified delineation agreement has to date been deposited with the United Nations.[2] The conventionally accepted boundary was a result primarily of negotiations in which the British high commissioner to Iraq, Sir Percy Cox, unilaterally drew dividing lines upon his imperial map to distinguish Iraq, Saudi Arabia, and Kuwait.[3] Referring to these talks in a letter to the ruler of Kuwait on 17 February 1921, Cox stated:

> The line starts from the southern bank of the mouth of Khaur az-Zubair and, with the town of Kuwait as centre, describes a semicircle, and, passing to the south of Quarian meets the sea just south of Ras al-Qualiyah, opposite Qaru Island. H.M. Government considers that [this area], in view of this Convention, belongs to the Shaikh of Kuwait beyond dispute.[4]

One of Cox's innovations was to construct two neutral zones on the Saudi border (one with Iraq, the other with Kuwait), which served as a compromise between flexible frontiers and strict boundaries that resulted in shared sovereignty.[5] The Saudi Arabia–Kuwait Neutral Zone, 2,500 square miles in all, was the subject of successful negotiations between the two countries in the 1960s, in which the neutral zone was divided into two equal parts by a single straight line. Likewise, the Iraqi–Saudi Arabia Neutral Zone is said to have been divided by agreement in 1975. Nonetheless, this latter zone is still a feature of contemporary maps, while the former retains some economic and political import.[6]

When Iraq accepted Kuwait's sovereignty and independence in 1963 (two years after sovereignty had been granted by Britain and first challenged by Iraq), the Agreed Minutes codifying that acceptance referred—

in an act of continuous regression to other texts—to correspondence of 1932 between Iraq and Kuwait. Neither the 1932 letters nor the 1963 minutes, however, contained any map of triangulation or demarcation to specify clearly the border's location. Although Britain in 1951 offered an interpretation of the 1932 correspondence, the interpretation was extremely vague (containing locational references such as "just south of Safwan") and was ignored, furthermore, by the 1963 negotiations.[7]

To try and clarify matters and resolve the dispute between Iraq and Kuwait, the Arab League in 1962 established a Military Patrol Line (MPL) straddled by a buffer zone that was to be free of provocative activities. In contravention of the league's agreement, Kuwait moved drilling rigs into that zone in the 1970s; Iraqi troops then crossed the MPL to drive them back. The ensuing standoff lasted until the early 1980s, when Kuwait moved back in to establish a dozen drilling sites while Iraq was at war with Iran. Establishing a claim to the area, rather than achieving access to the oil per se, motivated the Kuwaitis' actions, because at 12,000 barrels per day, oil from the disputed zone constituted less than one-half of 1 percent of Kuwait's total production.[8]

As a result of the Gulf War, another attempt is being made to settle upon an agreed border between the two countries. The United Nations Iraq-Kuwait Observation Mission (UNIKOM)—set up by UN Security Council Resolution 678 of 3 April 1991 as part of the conditions of the ceasefire—has responsibility for finally inscribing the Kuwait boundary.[9] The process for establishing an international border involves three stages: it has to be "allocated" (agreement reached as to the zone it will pass through); "delimited" (the specific position drawn on a map); and "demarcated" (the position marked on the ground). In a featureless area such as the Arabian peninsula, the third requirement is both particularly important and particularly difficult.[10] UNIKOM, which is patrolling a 9.3-mile demilitarized zone akin to the Arab League's 1962 Military Patrol Line, established the Iraq-Kuwait Boundary Demarcation Commission to fulfill its responsibility. The result, however, has in all probability laid the groundwork for a future conflict. Reports of the commission's findings indicate that the border will be moved several thousand yards north, giving Kuwait half a dozen additional wells in the disputed Rumaila oil field and half of the Iraqi port and naval base at Umm Qasr. As a result, Kuwait will have obtained all that it claimed from Iraq in the 1970s and 1980s.[11]

The Iraqi-Kuwaiti border, therefore, shares much of the arbitrariness and contingency associated with boundary lines in former colonial possessions. But its problematic status in this regard has been compounded. Whereas in Africa, for example, there has been a deliberate decision on the part of all sovereign authorities to accept and abide by the colonial demarcations, thereby ensuring their existence through mutual recognition, the Iraqi-Kuwaiti border is marked by a conspicuous absence of mutual recognition: one or other side has always actively contested the line. Moreover, this situation has been exacerbated by the work of the Iraq-Kuwait Boundary Demarcation Commission. Although Iraq had one representative on the commission, it withheld endorsement of the proposed line, thereby assuring the continued absence of mutual recognition.

If the territorial boundary between Iraq and Kuwait was unclear, the place of Iraq within U.S. policy toward the Persian Gulf countries between 1982 and 1990 was not. U.S.-Iraqi policy was part of a large and infinitely complex web of relations in which were linked the question of U.S. hostages in Lebanon, elements of the Iran-Contra scandal, and events and issues that later came to be understood as Iraqgate.[12] Whatever the details of the relationships in question, as a recipient of overt and covert economic, diplomatic, and military assistance from the United States and its allies during that time, Iraq was considered to be something other than an agent of evil.

DOING BUSINESS

The Affair Begins

Relations between the United States and Iraq, severed in the wake of the 1967 Six Day War in the Middle East, improved in the 1980s in response to the Reagan administration's concern about Iran's progress in the first Gulf War.[13] In addition to the existing overt effort to maintain an arms embargo against Iran (Operation Staunch), the United States instituted a number of initiatives to aid Iraq directly. It seems that after a secret visit by then CIA Director William Casey to Baghdad in 1982, the United States began permitting third parties (including Egypt, Jordan, Saudi Arabia, and, ironically, Kuwait) to transfer U.S. military hardware to Iraq with the knowledge that their stocks would then be replenished. The United States also indicated to its Western allies, particularly the French, that it concurred with their desire to sell Iraq high-technology weaponry.[14] In addition, the Iraqi military was permitted to see U.S. intelligence photographs and reports on the Iranian military and its positions.

Even though the Reagan administration aided and abetted Iran's military through covert channels until 1986 (the Iran-Contra affair), the United States began to tilt heavily toward Iraq once Iran captured the Faw peninsula (situated only twenty-five miles from Kuwait) in 1987. Intelligence and satellite data were passed to the Iraqis in increasing quantities. Moreover, the United States played an increasingly direct role in the use of this information. U.S. intelligence officers not only interpreted the information and plotted the coordinates of Iranian troop movements for the Iraqis; they recommended various targets to them. Indeed, two U.S. Navy ships (the *Stark* and the *Coontz*) were stationed in the Gulf to radio those coordinates and suggested targets to Iraqi units in the field. The incident in which the USS *Stark* was hit by an Iraqi missile on 17 May 1987 was caused, one analyst suggests, when that missile mistakenly homed in on the radio beam transmitted from the *Stark* that was directing the Iraqi pilot toward his Iranian target. Thirty-seven sailors died as a result of that incident, but the Reagan administration quickly accepted an Iraqi apology and offer of compensation. Furthermore, the incident prompted the United States to intensify its antagonism with Iran, resulting in a ten-fold increase in the U.S. naval presence in the Gulf. It was at this juncture that Kuwaiti oil tankers were reflagged and escorted by the U.S. Navy, an initiative that directly aided Iraq by securing sea lanes and port access vital to Iraqi resupply efforts. This was only one of a number of moves that led Iran to fear a direct attack from the United States. In fact, one instance might have been designed to confirm that impression: at the moment when Iraqi forces were mobilizing to retake the Faw peninsula, U.S. forces staged a military maneuver in the direction of the Straits of Hormuz as a distraction.[15] Moreover, while it had been asserted—most notably during the confirmation hearings of Robert Gates as director of Central Intelligence—that the intelligence relationship with Iraq had effectively concluded with the Iran-Iraq ceasefire in August 1988, it was subsequently disclosed that the arrangement was still in effect as of 24 May 1990 and that it had not been dissolved prior to Iraq's invasion of Kuwait.[16] Other military assistance programs were also considered in the spring of 1990: only three months before the invasion of Kuwait, proposals were afoot in the Pentagon to train Iraqi soldiers.[17]

There were also a number of covert programs in place designed directly to bolster the capability of the Iraqi military. Since 1979, Argentina, Egypt, and Iraq had been cooperating in the Condor missile project, the intention of which was to produce an intermediate-range ballistic missile capable of delivering both conventional and unconventional warheads.[18] Technology for this project was derived from a number of Western companies, most notably Messerschmitt-Bolkow-Blohm of Germany, but including as well thirteen U.S. firms.[19] During the 1980s, in contravention of the United Nations' comprehensive arms embargo against South Africa, the CIA permitted unlicensed exports of ballistic missile technology from one U.S. firm (International Signal and Control of Lancaster, Pennsylvania) to South Africa and Chile. This technology was subsequently—again with CIA knowledge—passed on to Iraq for use in the Condor program.[20] Federal investigators subsequently confirmed the CIA's role in this affair, highlighting one of the many ironies associated with U.S. policy toward Iraq: intelligence agencies were playing a role in a program that other branches of the U.S. administration were making a considerable effort to end. In May 1991 the United States finally succeeded in pressuring the Argentineans to end participation in the Condor program, effectively leading to its demise, but concerns remain that the full extent of cooperation between Argentina and Iraq has yet to be disclosed.[21]

In a similar vein, the CIA was apparently aware of illegal exports of cyanide from a factory in Florida (established by an Iraqi businessman who had been involved in the construction of Libya's chemical facility at Rabata) destined for Iraq's chemical weapons program.[22] Likewise, it has recently been alleged that some of Iraq's SCUD launchers—which were the object of considerable concern and attention during Desert Storm—were manufactured by a U.S. company (KCS of Westport, Connecticut). Although the physical manufacture of these trucks took place at a subsidiary company in Motherwell, Scotland (the Terex Corporation), it is claimed by some officials of the firm that the export of these trucks was made with the full knowledge of both the CIA and British intelligence.[23] If this were the case, it would be consistent with the fact that British intelligence officials, with the connivance of senior government ministers in the United Kingdom, also approved of and perhaps encouraged military-related exports to Iraq through machine tool companies such as Matrix-Churchill.[24] The revelation of such details has led one observer to note that Iraqgate can be considered "the first global political scandal."[25]

Increasing Support

An important aftereffect of William Casey's 1982 visit to Baghdad was that Iraq was removed from the State Department's list of nations that sponsor or support terrorist activities. Although the Justice Department was aware that there had been no change in Iraqi policy to justify such a move, the fact that Lieutenant Colonel Oliver North of the National Security Council was in charge of antiterrorism policy meant that any attempt by the Justice Department to begin prosecutions of Iraqi-based terrorist groups would be stymied.[26] This change in U.S. policy allowed Iraq to benefit from a range of U.S. financial aid programs, such that between 1983 and 1990 Iraq received over $5 billion in Agriculture Department credit guarantees (through the Commodity Credit Corporation) for the purchase of U.S. produce.[27] The importance of these measures must not be underestimated, because they came at a time when commercial sources of unsecured credit for Iraq had dried up; major banks regarded the country as such a risk they were quoting interest rates of between 15 and 25 percent on any loans that were not government supported.[28]

The basis for this policy was National Security Directive 26, signed by President Bush in October 1989, which mandated the provision of economic and political incentives as the means to moderate the regime of Saddam Hussein and support U.S. interests.[29] This presidential order, the bulk of which remains classified, has been the subject of controversy for two reasons. The first is that it was signed even when there were substantial concerns about the way Iraq had used previous credits and the ends they were serving. In an internal State Department memorandum of October 1989, officials were warned that "although additional research needs to be done, it appears more and more likely that CCC-guaranteed funds and/or commodities may have been diverted from Iraq to third parties in exchange of military hardware."[30] The memorandum continued:

> The unfolding BNL [Banca Nazionale del Lavoro; see below] scandal is directly involved with the Iraqi CCC program and cannot be separated from it. Of the $4 billion of unauthorized loans involved, about $1 billion were CCC guaranteed. Treasury and the Fed., however, find it hard to believe that Iraqi Central Bank officials and others were not aware of kickbacks and other gross irregularities.[31]

Nor were these documents the only warnings expressed within the administration about the consequences of financial and technological aid for Iraq. As far back as March 1985 it was clear to the Pentagon that Iraq's interest in acquiring nuclear weapons and in generally expanding its military capability meant there was "a real possibility" that U.S. technology would be diverted to those ends.[32] Moreover, it has been revealed that in November 1989—three months after the disclosure of the BNL funding pipeline and just days before the decision to grant Iraq further credit assistance—the White House received a CIA report on Iraqi military procurement, disclosing both the magnitude of Iraq's network and the BNL's role in it.[33] Subsequent disclosures demonstrate that there were a number of such warnings between June and September 1989, all of which preceded Bush's signing of NSD-26 and the granting of further financial aid to Iraq.[34]

The second point of controversy is that the U.S. credit guarantees were procured only after the most senior figures in the administration lobbied hard to grant them on foreign policy grounds. For example, the Export-Import Bank was pressured by Reagan administration officials (including then Vice-President Bush) to extend credit programs and insurance for U.S. corporations wanting to do business with Iraq, even though officials in the bank considered Iraq to be a major credit risk.[35] In the end, the bank provided $267 million in assistance for nearly two hundred business transactions with Iraq. After Congress passed a legislative prohibition on the bank's program with Iraq in December 1989, the Bush administration overrode the prohibition in February 1990, on grounds that it served the national interest to do so, but Iraq's poor credit record kept it from receiving bank assistance.[36] Furthermore, Secretary of State James Baker was personally involved in interventions with other members of the administration, which were designed to assuage doubts about Iraq and to insure the commitment of funds in support of Iraq. The most important outcome of his interventions was the granting of an additional $1 billion in loan guarantees in late 1989, even after considerable doubts had been expressed at lower levels in the administration. Although only half of this package was made available to Iraq in early 1990, officials in the State Department and National Security Council were pushing to deliver the second half as late as July 1990. Once these dealings were revealed, President Bush stated that he remained proud of his role and actively contested the idea that there was any evidence that Iraq was misusing the loans enabled by the credit guarantees.[37] Some Democratic lawmakers responded to these claims by alleging the existence of a cover-up involving the alteration of documents submitted to Congress by senior officials in the executive branch; these legislators called for the appointment of an independent counsel to examine the issue, a move initially rejected by the Bush Justice Department.[38]

However, in October 1992, after having been subjected to considerable pressure during the presidential campaign, Attorney General Barr appointed a special counsel to investigate the issue. That investigation uncovered sufficient indication of wrongdoing by administration officials to warrant, according to the special counsel, Judge Frederick Lacey, an expanded independent counsel inquiry.[39] Allegations made in the course of the investigation raised the possibility that the CIA concealed information on the BNL scandal from the court in Atlanta hearing the case against BNL officials, that senior officials in the Bush administration restricted the access congressional investigators had to relevant documents on policy with Iraq, and that a number of the documents that were supplied had been altered to conceal the administration's knowledge of the military value of exports to Iraq.[40]

Another effect of the change in Iraq's status subsequent to 1982 was that it removed additional foreign policy controls from the normal Commerce Department licensing program for technology exports. In 1987, two years after shipments had begun, then Vice-President Bush met with the Iraqi ambassador in Washington to assure him that previously unavailable technology could be purchased by Iraq.[41] Actions supported his contention. Between 1985 and 1990, 771 export licenses to Iraq for "dual-use technology" (civilian products that might have military applications) worth $1.5 billion were approved.[42] Some of the products shipped were extraordinary. Eighteen of those licenses were for toxins or bacteria (though such trade was curtailed when additional export controls on biological agents were promulgated by the Commerce Department in February 1989); others allowed the export of precursor chemicals necessary in the manufacture of mustard gas (for example, Alcolac, a Baltimore-based company, sold Iraq five hundred tons of thiodiglycol);[43] while eighty-two involved goods sent openly to military end-users—including computers to the Iraqi atomic energy agency, jet technology to its defense department, and personal security equipment for the Iraqi president.[44] Even when some of the companies themselves expressed concern to the Commerce Department about the possible application of the technology they were proposing to export, those worries were dismissed.[45]

Of course, U.S. companies were not alone in their willingness to trade with Iraq. Between 1982 and 1989 German corporations exported approximately $650 million worth of technology to Iraq, much of it with obvious military applications.[46] Likewise, corporations from numerous other European and Middle Eastern countries have been identified as prominent participants in the trade with Iraq.[47]

Civilian or Military?

During the Gulf War, the fragile distinction between civilian and military infrastructure was more often than not erased by the coalition's bombing strategy. Similarly, in prewar relations between Iraq and the West, the distinction between what constituted civilian trade and what constituted military trade was often blurred. Consider, for example, the proposal by a joint venture corporation comprising America's General Motors and Sweden's Volvo (along with three other U.S. firms: Cummins Engine Company, Eaton Corporation, and Rockwell Corporation) to build a facility to manufacture five thousand heavy vehicles per year in Iraq.[48] An internal memorandum from the Volvo GM Heavy Truck Corporation noted that their negotiations in Baghdad revealed that "the responsibility for industrialization of Iraq has been placed with the Iraqi Army"; that the delegation with whom they met was headed by a brigadier general; that the ministry involved had charge of both industry and armaments; and that during their tour they were shown top-secret defense operations in Iraq.[49] However, none of this deterred the businessmen from proceeding. In the end, though, the failure of the United States Export-Import Bank to extend credit guarantees to the participants seems to have killed the project.

It is in the realm of international business where issues of agency are often at their most complex. The bureaucratic complexities of a government can diminish the capacity of any single voice to be the official

representative of the state—when, for example, a commerce department
favors a transaction that a defense department opposes, while an intelligence agency pursues an altogether different course. Moreover, the struc-
ture of international capital equally disaggregates the issue of agency in
the nongovernmental realm. In many of the transactions with Iraq that
have come under scrutiny since the Gulf War, tracing the contours of
agency to establish the lines of authority, responsibility, and sovereignty
is fraught with complications, thereby unsettling the ethical border the
Bush administration constructed between "us" and "them." In one congressional inquiry, investigators relied upon the conviction that one can
"classify companies by the country in which they are headquartered."[50]
Yet if one looks at Iraq's corporate investments in Europe, the notion of
an easily identifiable headquarters is dubious.

For example, an Iraqi shareholding in the French media group Ha-
chette was made by Montana Management Incorporated, a Panamanian-
registered holding vehicle. Montana, however, is controlled by Midco
Financial, a Geneva-based company, headed by an Iraqi who is also
president of Montana.[51] Where does one locate corporate sovereignty and
state regulatory responsibility? Likewise, if we consider Iraq's purchase
of computers for missile wind tunnel experiments, we see that three
countries and five companies were agents at one stage or another. Two
major components were sent from their manufacturers, Gould in Florida
and Electronics Associates in New Jersey, to a British firm, Scientific
Computers, which connected them and sent them on to that firm's German subsidiary, EAI of Aachen. EAI then transferred them to another
German company, Messerschmitt-Bolkow-Blohm, which coordinated
many exports to Iraq and which dispatched the computers in question to
to the Saad 16 military complex outside Baghdad.[52]

The BNL Scandal

The question of agency and responsibility in the West's relationship
with Iraq becomes even more complex when one considers that many of
these commercial transactions were financed by banks operating in gray
areas. In particular, the activities of the Banca Nazionale Del Lavoro at
its Atlanta, Georgia office highlight the way in which much of the commerce with Iraq, corporate as well as state-based, was conducted covertly.
BNL, government-owned and the largest of Italian banks, was Iraq's
primary source of Western loans in the period between 1987 and 1989.
While other banks refused to risk business with Iraq, BNL Atlanta provided over $4 billion through more than 2,500 letters of credit.[53] Half of
that money funded agricultural purchases, many of which were guaranteed by the U.S. Department of Agriculture's Commodity Credit Corpo-

ration, while the remaining half was provided to three Iraqi government banks for the purchase of technology. Some of that money was paid directly to exporters in the United States and Europe, but most of it was disbursed through a procedure in which BNL Atlanta shifted money from its New York accounts in U.S. banks to Iraqi accounts in similar banks, after which it was paid to various corporations.[54] BNL Atlanta's ability to provide Iraq with such substantial funding was made possible by its triple-A credit rating, enabling it to construct what was essentially a pyramid operation, in which it borrowed short-term loans from one bank and then raised additional funds on the money market to pay them off when due, before borrowing again.[55]

The loans provided Iraq by BNL Atlanta funded a wide range of dual-use technology and military hardware, including elements of the Condor missile program, the ill-fated supergun project, and the nuclear triggers seized in London just prior to export in May 1990.[56] Although some officials in BNL's Rome headquarters referred customers hoping to do business with Iraq to its Atlanta branch, both the scale and scope of the BNL Atlanta operation were contrary to the official financial restrictions imposed by the Rome head office.[57] With its loans to Iraq hidden through off-the-book accounting, BNL Atlanta was able to circumvent both its internal corporate restrictions and bank regulators in the United States. It seems unlikely, however, that this operation would have escaped the attention of all U.S. authorities or its Rome managers. Indeed, when BNL headquarters wanted the Atlanta branch to cease participation in the CCC agricultural loans to Iraq, a former BNL Atlanta official recalled, the branch was "very, very heavily encouraged by the [U.S.] government to stay in the program."[58] Moreover, since the CIA tracked (and tacitly condoned) some aspects of the Condor missile program, and since other branches of the intelligence community were unlikely to have been oblivious to the movement of billions of dollars out of the country, it is possible that in one way or another BNL Atlanta had received at least a covert imprimatur from elements of the U.S. government for military-related loans, a suspicion reinforced by the revelation that intelligence documents as far back as 1986 show the BNL operation was under surveillance.[59] Indeed, Dr. Norman Bailey, a former National Security Agency staffer and specialist in tracking international money flows, has stated that "the likelihood of a branch of an Italian bank in Atlanta, Georgia dealing with the kind of sums that were involved not coming to the attention of U.S. authorities would be almost zero."[60] Given this, Bailey concluded, "The only explanation I can think of is that the authorities knew all about it and approved it. . . . They were using this as a channel for the financing of certain activities."[61] In a remark consistent with the idea that the BNL operation was an officially known element of Iraqui policy, the State

Department reportedly told investigators that it was not a "rogue opera-tion,"[62] while a report from the Italian senate—although citing only cir-cumstantial evidence—has argued that it is not credible that the operation was conducted without official knowledge at the least.[63]

This contention is supported by two U.S. government memos (one from the New York Federal Reserve in October 1989, the other from the Agriculture Department in February 1990) revealing that some officials were aware that BNL had financed "companies allegedly involved in manufacturing and exporting parts and technology to Iraq for the Condor 2 missile project."[64] Furthermore, once the BNL Atlanta operation was exposed in late August 1989 (there is some suggestion that its existence was disclosed by Israeli authorities), the attorney general, the State De-partment, and the Office of Legal Counsel in the White House all inter-vened in one way or another with the U.S. attorney's office in Atlanta to retard the grand jury investigation. The indictments of BNL officials were held up for over a year by the State Department's insistence that President Hussein not be offended. The secretary of state contacted Iraqi officials about the issue in September or October of 1989, and the BNL operation was the subject of many telexes between April Glaspie, the U.S. ambas-sador to Iraq, and Washington.[65]

One other aspect of the BNL scandal reveals the difficulties in speci-fying agency and locating responsibility, and highlights the way in which public/private distinctions are difficult to sustain in U.S. foreign policy circles. Two senior administration officials, national security advisor Brent Scowcroft and Deputy Secretary of State Lawrence Eagleburger, did work for BNL while they were employed with Henry Kissinger's prominent consulting firm. Although they claim their links with BNL were tenuous at best, congressional Democrat Henry Gonzalez has charged that they should have disqualified themselves from the debate within the adminis-tration over the CCC program with Iraq.[66] Other links also existed: Henry Kissinger himself was on BNL's international advisory committee be-tween 1985 and 1991 (he told the Financial Times that he resigned in February 1991, although he did not actually depart until August of that year)[67] while a Kissinger Associates executive was a prominent member of the delegation from the U.S.-Iraq Business Forum that met with Saddam Hussein in Baghdad in June 1989.[68] Similarly, two additional instances of potential conflicts of interest have been associated with this case: President Bush's nominee for U.S. attorney in Miami had previously represented a Chilean arms dealer who has come under investigation by that office for secret deals with Iraq, while the new U.S. attorney for Atlanta—in charge of the office investigating BNL—was previously counsel to an Iraqi front com-pany (Matrix Churchill) closely connected to BNL.[69]

The complex, multifarious, sometimes overt, sometimes covert nature of the international/intercorporate relations that existed among Iraq, the United States, and its Western allies, makes it impossible to draw any clear boundary that would clarify where agency and responsibility reside in the transfer of technology to Iraq. Governments, corporations, and components of both have at various times entered into often conflicting alliances and arrangements either to promote or to prohibit relations with Iraq (which is itself a less than unified subject). When confronted with a record like this awash in shades of gray, it takes some effort to see the picture in terms of black and white. Indeed, it is precisely when confronted with this much ambiguity that a discourse of moral certitude is incessantly summoned to bring order and allocate responsibility. Nonetheless, with an undisturbed faith in the principle of sovereignty, President Bush was unperturbed by the charge that the U.S. response to the Iraqi invasion might have been hypocritical:

> And it is true that our administration and others previously tried to work with Iraq. But this brutal aggression—what they did here is such a clear violation of international law that the entire world was united in opposition to it. So, if there was a mistake made in trying to move them along a more civilized path by having contacts as we did, fine. But this kind of revisionistic view that that makes what's happening today wrong—I'm sorry, I don't agree with it at all.[70]

Furthermore, during the 1992 presidential campaign, Bush tried to deny the mounting evidence of both direct and indirect U.S. commercial and governmental assistance to Iraq by declaring, "To allege that we were building up his [Saddam Hussein's] arms or building up his nuclear power knowingly is simply fallacious."[71]

Just as the United States absolved itself from the consequences and implications of the network of economic, diplomatic, and military relationships between itself and Iraq in the prewar period, so too did it overlook or ignore (even though it may have been involved in) the grievances that gave rise to the Iraqi invasion of Kuwait.

FERMENTING GRIEVANCES

Money, Oil, and the Balance of Power

On the eve of the war with Iraq, the U.S Congress authorized the president to use military force in the Gulf. Aside from the fact that the vote was far from being overwhelming, the joint congressional resolution invoked two assumptions that warrant critical review. The first was the view, expressed in the resolution's opening paragraph, that "the Government of Iraq without provocation invaded" Kuwait.72 Indeed, spoken or unspoken, this was the most basic assumption at work in the U.S. response to the crisis. Whenever advocates of military action spoke of the events of August 1990, their sentences were peppered with phrases declaring that Iraq's action was a "flagrant" act, "clear and unambiguous," the "brazenness" of which "violated . . . fundamental norms" with "utter disregard," and so on.73 These formulations figured the invasion of 2 August 1990 in terms of the World War II script (Bush spoke of a "blitzkrieg" attack),74 rendering it a complete bolt from the blue, an event without context, and an act without history. While it is certainly not my intention to argue that events prior to 2 August 1990 condone or justify Iraq's military invasion and occupation of Kuwait (an argument that would simply reverse rather than fundamentally contest the way in which the responsibility for evil has been located in these events), I do want to consider factors that contextualize the invasion in a way that renders predominant interpretations more ambiguous.

Iraq's relations with its Gulf and Arab neighbors—much like the West's relations with Iraq—revolved around Iran. Having begun a war with Iran in 1980, Iraq understood itself to be fighting a long and bloody conflict in the service of others, to contain what was generally represented as an expansionist Islamic fundamentalism. Having shouldered responsibility as a regional mercenary for the anti-Khomeni coalition, Iraq considered itself to have earned by 1988 the necessary capital (political and monetary) from its neighbors for the extensive reconstruction of its society that the ceasefire with Iran enabled.

During the eight-year war with Iran, Iraq had largely ceased exporting oil and had thus greatly diminished its export earnings. Indeed, Iraq arranged for the oil-producing states in the Gulf—including Kuwait—to take over its OPEC quota of three million barrels per day, thereby giving them a windfall in additional revenue. In return, some of those states lent Iraq a considerable amount of money ($22 billion in the case of Kuwait) to finance its war with Iran.[75] Interestingly, part of Kuwait's aid to Iraq during the war with Iran came in the form of cash grants earned through sales of oil produced in the Kuwait-Saudi Arabia Neutral Zone and sold on Iraq's account.[76] But while some states, including Saudi Arabia, removed their loans to Iraq from the books—thereby effectively treating them as gifts and improving Iraq's international credit worthiness—Kuwait declined to do so and insisted on repayment from Iraq.[77] Although this was a more than considerable irritant in relations between the two countries in the period leading up to August 1990, it was exacerbated by Kuwait's aggressive policy aimed at increasing its share of OPEC-mandated production quotas.

The day after the ceasefire between Iraq and Iran in August 1988, Kuwait unilaterally decided to violate existing OPEC agreements and increase its level of oil production. Aside from lowering world oil prices—a move the Iraqis calculated would cost them $7 billion per year from their recently resumed exports—the decision involved pumping more oil from the disputed Rumaila oil field, two-thirds of which has been said to lie within Iraqi territory.[78] In March 1989 Kuwait announced another challenge, with a proposal to expand its production quota by 50 percent, a move rejected by the June 1989 OPEC meeting. Kuwait's response was to declare immediately that it was no longer bound by OPEC quotas, a point it demonstrated by doubling its production from one to two million barrels per day. When the United Arab Emirates followed suit, world oil prices plunged to a new low, further reducing the level of oil revenues earned by countries like Iraq.[79] Some sources in the Middle East believed that in following this strategy of collapsing oil prices, the Gulf states were trying to bring down or contain Iraq in a manner similar to the way they had successfully weakened Iran during the Iran-Iraq war.[80]

Unable to obtain substantial sources of credit from international banks because of its poor credit history (the BNL Atlanta conduit excepted), and under pressure from falling oil prices, Iraq began to air its grievances publicly. Beginning with the 24 February 1990 Arab Cooperation Council meeting in Baghdad, President Hussein engaged in a series of angry analyses of world and regional events, which included the demand that Gulf oil states provide some $30 billion in new loans and finances for Iraq's industrial reconstruction.[81] This political offensive continued throughout subsequent months. At an Arab summit on 3 May, President Hussein alleged that for every dollar the world price of oil fell, Iraq lost $1 billion per year in revenue. Finally, on 16 July Iraq took the unusual step of publicly presenting an extensive list of grievances against Kuwait to the Arab League and sought a response.[82]

The U.S. Position

Throughout this period, there were a number of contacts between the United States and Iraq, most notably President Hussein's respective meetings with a Senate delegation on 12 April 1990 and with Ambassador April Glaspie on 25 July. On these occasions U.S. officials were appraised of the problem and articulated a number of disparate responses. These ranged from Ambassador Glaspie's and Assistant Secretary of State Kelly's declarations that the United States had no opinion on inter-Arab border disputes and was without obligations to Kuwait, to a joint military exercise in July 1990 with the United Arab Emirates in response to President Hussein's public pronouncements.[83] During the meeting with

Glaspie, the Iraqi president noted that some progress toward a solution of the issue had been made through the mediation of Egyptian President Mubarak. Others, including PLO leader Yassir Arafat and Jordanian King Hussein, were also involved in extensive behind-the-scenes negotiations to try and diffuse the growing rift between Iraq and the Gulf states. The culmination of these efforts was a planned summit involving Iraq, Saudi Arabia, and Kuwait, to be held in the Saudi city of Jeddah on 31 July. At the same time, Iraqi troops were said to be massing on the Kuwaiti border.

Given the conventional understanding that Arab summits do not occur unless an agreement has been worked out, a number of sources indicate that a plan had been formulated by which Kuwait (and possibly Saudi Arabia) would offer Iraq $10 billion in new finances, and by which other outstanding issues would also be resolved.[84] What actually took place at this meeting remains something of a mystery, but no one doubts that it ultimately failed and precipitated the Iraqi invasion of Kuwait. Some accounts say that Kuwait was intransigent and unprepared to deal with Iraq, others maintain that the Iraqis were arrogant and insulting toward the Kuwaitis, and still others say that progress was made on the question of new finances but scuttled by inflexibility on other issues.[85]

Whatever the details of the Jeddah summit, there remains the question of whether or not Britain and/or the United States exerted any direct or indirect influence on Kuwait that shaped its approach to the conflict with Iraq. A number of accounts suggest that Kuwait may have been emboldened by Britain and the United States to take a hard line with the Iraqis and refuse any concessions. One senior BBC reporter claims that during a July 1990 meeting between Yassir Arafat and the Kuwaiti crown prince, in which the two leaders sought a resolution to the crisis, the prince received a phone call from then British Prime Minister Thatcher, urging the Kuwaitis to stand firm and reject all of Iraq's claims with the knowledge that both Britain and the United States would fully back them should the need arise.[86] Another account maintains that the Kuwaiti crown prince revealed at the Jeddah summit that he had an assurance from the British that Iraq would not attack.[87] Still other reports note that in his instructions to his crown prince before the Jeddah summit, the Kuwaiti emir told him to resist Iraqi demands, noting that this conformed with "the opinion of our friends in Egypt, Washington, and London."[88] Furthermore, Crown Prince Hassan of Jordan stated during a January 1991 interview that the Kuwaitis had unofficially told Jordan that the United States would come to their aid in any confrontation with Iraq.[89]

The view that the United States, Britain, and Kuwait colluded to some extent in their relations with Iraq—whether inadvertently or deliberately—finds support from other sources. Following their invasion of Kuwait, the Iraqis released a document they claim to have found in the

Kuwaiti Ministry of Foreign Affairs, in which the Kuwaiti director-general of state security writes of a 14 November 1989 meeting with CIA Director William Webster at which possible coordination between the Kuwaitis and the United States was discussed. Paragraph five of this report reads:

> We agreed with the American side that it was important to take advantage of the deteriorating economic situation in Iraq in order to put pressure on that country's government to delineate our common border. The Central Intelligence Agency gave us its view of appropriate means of pressure, saying that broad cooperation should be initiated between us, on condition that such activities are coordinated at a high level.[90]

The CIA released a statement on 30 October 1990 (after the document was made public) declaring that it was a forgery, although the agency did confirm that there had been a meeting between officials of the Kuwaiti state security organization and the CIA director in November 1989.[91] The CIA denial, however, was so careful and specific—stating that there was no discussion at the meeting on 14 November 1989—that it led one commentator to wonder if a proposal for applying pressure to Iraq had been raised by Kuwaiti officials at another meeting or with other officials.[92]

Whether or not the document itself was authentic, it was considered by Jordan's King Hussein to reflect the thrust of U.S. and Kuwaiti policy toward Iraq.[93] Indeed, it is possible to interpret later events as suggesting the plausibility of a U.S.-inspired plan to provoke Iraq. After all, the continuing pressure for intrusive UN inspections has been designed to irritate President Hussein and provide a pretext for justifying new U.S. overt and covert actions against Iraq. It is in this context that we can understand the renewed military strikes against Iraq in the final days of the Bush administration. As one U.S. official has said, "The whole program of the inspection regime is to keep putting sand in his shorts."[94]

The central proposition of the purported Kuwait-CIA document—that the Kuwaitis economically pressure Iraq into delineating their common border—has been a fundamental tenet of Kuwaiti policy toward Iraq since independence in 1961. Whenever pressed by the Iraqis for financial assistance, the Kuwaiti response has been to raise the issue of demarcating the border between the two countries; this exchange occurred on any number of occasions in the early 1960s, at the 1988 Arab summit in Algeria, after the Iraqis presented their written demands to the Arab League on 16 July 1990, and during the failed Jeddah summit on 31 July 1990.[95]

Of course, the contention that there had been a conspiracy between Kuwait and the West to pressure Iraq was a staple of Iraqi declarations as tensions escalated in the spring of 1990. For all the bluster of these pronouncements, however, there are—aside from the issues raised above—a number of circumstances that make the Iraqi interpretation viable and perhaps understandable. Having been favored with close relations and considerable assistance from Western nations in the 1980s, several changes in its situation, beginning in late 1988 (the period in which Kuwait was engaged in a strategy of aggressive oil diplomacy), suggested to Iraq that the tide was turning against it. Although there was nothing qualitatively different about Iraqi behavior to distinguish this period from others, Western attitudes and policies certainly began to change in the aftermath of the Iran-Iraq war. Between the fall of 1988 and early 1989 the Western nations began a campaign against chemical weapons, even though the same countries had been turning a blind eye toward Iraqi use since 1984. In May 1989 French arms sales to Iraq ended. Between January 1989 and August 1990 Western customs authorities began intercepting numerous pieces of high-technology equipment and weaponry bound for Iraq, although there had been no such seizures, despite numerous exports, in the previous period. In August 1989 the BNL Atlanta operation was raided and closed down; in October 1989 the U.S. Export-Import Bank ended guarantees for Iraq, and in May 1990 the U.S. Department of Agriculture announced an investigation into alleged Iraqi abuses of the CCC program.[96]

Other Possibilities

No matter how compelling the narrative—as outlined thus far—might seem in its accounting of the actors, events, and relationships intertwined in the period prior to the Iraqi invasion of Kuwait, other interpretations covering the same period are plausible. Indeed, the most common interpretation has been not that the United States incited Kuwait into an aggressive posture, but that it offered Iraq a green light for its invasion. By combining elements of April Glaspie's meeting with Saddam Hussein with Washington's failure throughout July 1990 to issue to Kuwait any overt statement of a security guarantee, many have argued that, intentionally or not, the Bush administration signaled to the Iraqi regime it would not respond to aggression. To this oft-cited scenario, the respected British newspaper *The Observer* has added a further element. During the build-up to the conflict in the second half of 1990, it was reported that a sometime emissary of the Bush administration had met with an Iraqi minister in New York in January of that year and discreetly suggested that to enhance its economic situation, Iraq should pursue through OPEC a determined strategy to push the price of oil up toward $25 per barrel.[97]

The details of these events and incidents are worthy of analysis in their own right, for they tell us much about the conduct and wisdom of various nations' foreign policy. Nonetheless, for our purposes here, the most important implication to be drawn from this interwoven web of Gulf diplomacy and interstate relations prior to August 1990 is that it does not easily lend itself to locating the responsibility for evil unambiguously in one agent as opposed to another. Given the complex and tension-ridden nexus of international, intercorporate, and interpersonal relations obtaining among Iraq, Iran, Kuwait, and the United States and its allies, setting the blame for the crisis of August 1990 at the feet of one party while absolving the other(s) of all responsibility is only possible by overlooking some legitimate factors while ignoring others altogether.

Ironically, given his judgment that the war with Iraq was just, Michael Walzer's articulation of just-war theory, notable for its unbending commitment to the importance of boundaries, makes allowance for a situation of the kind the Iraqis believed themselves to be facing. Having accepted the Israeli pre-emptive strike of 1967 as "a clear case of legitimate anticipation" warranted by the threat the Israelis perceived, Walzer argues that his theory of aggression therefore requires major revision.[98] While there are many more differences than similarities between the genesis of the Six Day War and that of the Iraq-Kuwait crisis, the implication Walzer draws from the former bears upon the latter, especially if one considers economic threats to be perilous to sovereignty:

> For it means that aggression can be made out not only in the absence of a military attack or invasion but in the (probable) absence of any immediate intention to launch such an attack or invasion. The general formula must go something like this: states may use military force in the face of threats of war, whenever the failure to do so would seriously risk their territorial integrity or political independence. Under such circumstances it can be fairly said that they have been forced to fight and that they are the victims of aggression.[99]

For the most part, however, partisans of the post-August 1990 U.S. position were content to dismiss even the possibility that legitimate grievances on the part of the Iraqis helped to ferment a crisis that culminated in the Iraqi invasion of Kuwait. As one writer declared, "Even if these charges were true, such actions [by Kuwait] clearly fell far short of the magnitude necessary to justify military retaliation. Rather conflicts of this sort are to be dealt with by negotiation and arbitration."[100] That diplomacy would have been the better route cannot be denied. But such declarations beg two questions. First, why was there not more support from the United States and its allies for the diplomatic efforts of those who assiduously explored nonmilitary solutions to the conflict *prior* to August 1990? Second, and more importantly, why was the conflict *after* August 1990 not amenable to the virtues of negotiation and arbitration?

NOTES

The epigraph that opens this chapter is quoted from "American Flier Shot Down in Iraq Recounts Horrors After Capture," *New York Times*, 11 June 1991, B5.

1. Simpson, *From the House of War*, xiii.

2. G. Henry M. Schuler, "Congress Must Take a Hard Look at Iraq's Charges Against Kuwait," *Los Angeles Times*, 2 December 1990, M4.

3. For documents pertaining to these issues, see, Lauterpacht et al. eds., *The Kuwait Crisis*, 45–50.

4. Quoted in Lauterpacht et al., eds., *The Kuwait Crisis*, 46.

5. Brown, *The Saudi Arabia–Kuwait Neutral Zone*, 53–66.

6. Prescott, *Political Frontiers and Boundaries*, 62, 277; and Lauterpacht et al., eds., *The Kuwait Crisis*, 57–60.

7. Schofield, "The Iraq-Kuwait Boundary," 22.

8. Schuler, "Congress Must Take a Hard Look at Iraq's Charges Against Kuwait"; and Anderson and Rashidian, *Iraq and the Continuing Middle East Crisis*, 102–103, 109. It was this situation that led Iraq to charge in 1990 that Kuwait had "stolen" $2.4 billion in oil.

9. Schofield, "The Iraq-Kuwait Boundary," 21.

10. Anderson and Rashidian, *Iraq and the Continuing Middle East Crisis*, 85.

11. "Is This Kuwait? No, This is Iraq. Really? Well, Not Exactly," *Wall Street Journal*, 5 December 1991, A1; "U.N. Carves Oilfield on Kuwaiti Border, Snipping Iraqi Share," *New York Times*, 17 April 1992, A10; "UN Group Grants Kuwait Part of Iraq's One Seaport," *Boston Globe*, 18 April 1992, 5; and "U.N. Map Makers Draw Kuwaiti-Iraqi Border," *Washington Post*, 5 May 1992, A19.

12. For details of the way in which these issues are interrelated, see Murray Waas and Craig Unger, "In the Loop: Bush's Secret Mission," *The New Yorker*, 2 November 1992; 64–83.

13. There have even been occasionally expressed suspicions that the United States—through a discussion that then national security advisor Zbigniew Brzezinski is alleged to have had with a senior Iraqi official in Jordan during July 1980—did not resist and could have encouraged Iraqi desires to engage in a conflict with Iran. Timmerman, *The Death Lobby*, 76–77. For an overview of U.S.-Iraqi relations in this period see Sciolino, *The Outlaw State*, especially Chapter 8. Recently declassified documents for the period between 1984 and 1990, although far from being a complete record of the thinking behind U.S. policy toward Iraq, strongly suggest that there was considerable internal debate as to its wisdom. "U.S. Documents Raise Questions Over Iraq Policy," *New York Times*, 7 June 1992, 1.

14. "U.S. Secretly Gave Aid to Iraq Early in Its War Against Iran," *New York Times*, 26 January 1992, 1; Murray Waas, "What Washington Gave Saddam for Christmas," in *The Gulf War Reader*, ed. Sifry and Cerf; Anthony Lewis, "Gangsters in Charge," *New York Times*, 22 April 1991, A17; and Timmerman, *The Death Lobby*, 192, 213. Details of the Saudi transfers—which both U.S. and Saudi officials claim were "inadvertent"—can be found in "White House Reportedly

Let Saudis Transfer U.S.-Made Arms to Saddam," *Washington Post*, 19 April 1992, A18; "Congress Probes Alleged Arms Transfers," *Washington Post*, 20 April 1992, A6; and "U.S. Says Saudis Sent U.S.-Made Arms to Iraq and 2 Other Nations," *New York Times*, 21 April 1992, A9.

15. Simpson, *From the House of War*, 40–46. Recent investigations have suggested that the USS *Vincennes*, the cruiser from which was fired the missile that shot down a civilian Iranian airliner, killing 290 people, adopted an openly aggressive posture designed to provoke the Iranians into conflict. See "U.S. Account of Downing of Iran Jet Criticized," *New York Times*, 2 July 1992, A7; and "Sea of Lies," *Newsweek*, 13 July 1992.

16. "US 'Shared Iran Intelligence with Saddam Hussein'," *Financial Times*, 10 March 1992, 4; "CIA Shared Data With Iraq Until Kuwait Invasion," *Washington Post*, 28 April 1992, A6.

17. "Pentagon Proposed Training Iraqis," *Los Angeles Times*, 4 August 1992, A4.

18. Sampson, *The Arms Bazaar in the Nineties*, 365; and Timmerman, *The Death Lobby*, 150154.

19. "Iraq Arms Aid Traced to U.S. Firms," *Los Angeles Times*, 4 February 1992, A4.

20. "CIA 'Allowed Illegal Export of US Missile Secrets'," *Financial Times*, 24 May 1991, 1; "Saddam's Secret South African Connection," *Financial Times*, 24 May 1991, 6.

21. "Bush's Choice of CIA Director Faces Obstacles," *Financial Times*, 11 June 1991, 7; "US Pressure to Cancel Missile Chafes Argentine Military," *Manchester Guardian Weekly*, 9 June 1991, 13; and "US Concerns Over Argentine Missile Links to Baghdad," *Financial Times*, 9 March 1992, 3.

22. "CIA Knew of Cyanide Exports to Iraq," *Financial Times*, 3 July 1991, 18; and "The Sinister Alchemy of the Iraqi 'Doctor'," *Financial Times*, 3 July 1991, 4.

23. "U.S. Linked to Iraqi Scud Launchers," *New York Times*, 26 January 1992, 12. The author of this story, Seymour Hersh, and his source, are now being sued by the Terex Corporation and KCS Industries in an effort to contest this report. "Firm Sues for Libel on Report on Iraq," *Boston Globe*, 18 April 1992, 4.

24. One of the British managers of Matrix Churchill, Paul Henderson—whose trial for violating export controls was abandoned in November 1992 after it was revealed that he was secretly encouraged by ministers in the Thatcher government—had a long history of cooperating with British intelligence. Commenting on why it was possible for Matrix Churchill to have been purchased by the Iraqis, Henderson observed, "There is no doubt in my mind that the business was sold to the Iraqis so we could monitor them." "Midlands Man Tells of Secret Life as Spy in Iraq," *Financial Times*, 10 November 1992, 9. For further details on this development, see "Spy Defends Briton in Arms Case," *Washington Post*, 4 November 1992, A39; "Secret Support for Saddam That Went to the Top," *Financial Times*, 10 November 1992, 9; "UK Arms to Iraq Court Case Collapses," *Financial Times*, 10 November 1992, 18; and "Profits Lured Britain to Accept Iraqi Deals," *Washington Post*, 24 November 1992, A1.

25. William Safire, "1st Global Political Scandal," *New York Times*, 12 November 1992, A25.

26. Lewis, "Gangsters in Charge." See also the account in Emerson and Del Sesto, *Terrorist*.

27. Statement by Representative Henry Gonzalez to the House of Representatives, 4 February 1991, *Congressional Record*, H845-H852.

28. Timmerman, *The Death Lobby,* 227.

29. "'89 Bush Order Says Ply Iraq With Aid," *New York Times,* 29 May 1992, 3. For an overview of the Bush policy, see Mark Hosenball, "The Odd Couple: How George Bush Helped Create Saddam Hussein," *The New Republic,* 1 June 1992.

30. Quoted in "State Dept. Aide to Testify on Iraq," *New York Times,* 21 June 1992, 15. See also "Documents Charge Prewar Iraq Swap: U.S. Food For Arms," *New York Times,* 27 April 1992, A1. There are indications that the State Department is now sensitive to the damaging nature of this document: when its author requested a copy from the department's files, it came to him with a cover note that read "Not in the system," indicating that it was to be removed from the available record. William Safire, "'Not in the System'," *New York Times,* 25 June 1992, A31.

31. Quoted in "U.S. Loans Indirectly Financed Iraq Military," *Los Angeles Times,* 25 February 1992, A1. The full text of this and other documents containing similar doubts and warnings have been placed on the public record by Congressman Henry Gonzalez of Texas. See Remarks by Gonzalez, 2 March 1992, *Congressional Record,* H858–H870; and Remarks by Gonzalez, 30 March 1992, *Congressional Record,* H2005–H2014.

32. "Documents Warned in '85 of Iraqi Nuclear Aims," *New York Times,* 5 July 1992, 10.

33. *Nightline,* 7 July 1992.

34. See "CIA Told White House of Iraqi Arms Efforts," *Los Angeles Times,* 6 August 1992, A1.

35. "Bush, Others Said to Have Repeatedly Pressed Bank to Aid Iraq," *Washington Post,* 25 February 1992, A13.

36. House Committee on Banking, Finance, and Urban Affairs, *Hearing on Iraqi and Banca Nazionale Del Lavoro Participation in Export-Import Programs,* 82–86.

37. "Secret Effort by Bush Helped Hussein Build Military Might," *Los Angeles Times,* 23 February 1992, A1; and "Bush Had Long Supported Aid for Iraq," *Los Angeles Times,* 24 February 1992, A1; "Baker Acted on Iraq Loan Guarantees," *Financial Times,* 3 March 1992, 7; "Bush Proud of Role in Secret Iraq Aid Policy," *Los Angeles Times,* 26 February 1992, A1; and "President Angrily Contests Charges Over Loans to Iraq," *New York Times,* 2 July 1992, A1.

38. "Cover-Up on Iraq is Charged to U.S.," *New York Times,* 24 June 1992, A7.

39. "Step Toward Special Prosecutor Is Taken in the Iraq Bank Inquiry," *New York Times,* 13 November 1992, A1.

40. On the allegations concerning the CIA—which have also embroiled the Justice Department and the FBI—see "Justice Department Role Cited in Deception on Iraq Loan Data," *New York Times,* 10 October 1992, 1; "C.I.A. and Justice Department Feud Over Inquiry in Iraq Loan Case," *New York Times,* 11 October 1992, A1; and "Justice Department Now Clashes With F.B.I. Over Inquiry into Bank Loans to Iraq," *New York Times,* 12 October 1992, A6. The actions of these various government agencies had led the federal judge trying the BNL case in Atlanta to call for the appointment of an independent prosecutor to investigate the issue. "Federal Judge Calls for Inquiry Into Bank's Loans to Iraq," *Los Angeles Times,* 3 June 1992, A8. On the allegations concerning the cover-up and alteration of documents within the Bush administration, see "Bush Aides Tied to Effort to Withhold Iraq Data," *Los Angeles Times,* 8 July 1992, A1; and "'Iraq Papers' Posed Threat to White House," *Los Angeles Times,* 19 July 1992, A1. ABC News

reported that the Commerce Department had altered sixty-eight documents. One of the simplest changes occurred when the word "military" was removed from the phrase "military trucks." *Nightline,* 28 October 1992.

41. "Secret Effort by Bush Helped Hussein Build Military Might."

42. Amazingly, at least one company seems to have been able to trade with Iraq through an Iraqi front company *after* the invasion of Kuwait. Records from Kennametal Incorporated of Latrobe, Pennsylvania show twenty-four transactions with Iraq-owned Matrix Churchill between August 1990 and March 1991. *Dateline NBC,* 7 April 1992.

43. House Committee on Banking, Finance, and Urban Affairs, *Hearing on Banca Nazionale Del Lavoro,* 90–91. Similarly licensed exports of chemicals took place between British companies and Iraq. "Iraq Nerve Gas Plant Uses DTI Listed Chemicals," *Financial Times,* 1 August 1991, 1. These exports were distinct from the illegal but covertly approved shipments referred to above.

44. House Subcommittee on International Economic Policy and Trade, *Hearing on United States Exports of Sensitive Technology to Iraq.* In the end, the total worth of the trade with Iraq approved by these licenses was between $500 million and $782 million, because a major deal to supply trucks fell through after its license was granted. "U.S. Tells of Prewar Technology Sales to Iraq Worth $500 Million," *New York Times,* 12 March 1991, A13; Waas, "What Washington Gave Saddam for Christmas," 90–91; "Memo Cites Exception on Iraqi Trade to Protect Hussein," *New York Times,* 23 May 1991, D5; and "Report Says US Exports to Iraq Aided Military," *Financial Times,* 20 June 1991, 3. See also Kenneth R. Timmerman, "Surprise! We Gave Hussein the Bomb," *New York Times,* 25 October 1991, A33; Gary Milhollin, "Building Saddam Hussein's Bomb," *New York Times Magazine,* 8 March 1992; and "Iraq's Bomb, Chip by Chip," *New York Times,* 24 April 1992, A32. It is possible that the number of licenses approved for exports to military end users was as high as 220. This figure was quoted by Representative Henry Gonzalez on *Nightline,* 28 October 1992.

45. For one company executive's account, see Henry M. Rowan, "Left Holding the Bag in Iraq," *New York Times,* 14 October 1992, A25.

46. Simpson, *From the House of War,* 214. For an overview of the German situation, see "A Country that Turned a Blind Eye," *Financial Times,* 25 March 1991, 20. To correct problems with German exports, authorities in that country have been making an effort to impose stricter controls and punish offenders. "Bonn Brings Poison Gas Charges," *Financial Times,* 13 March 1991, 2; and "Germany Acts to Curb Arms Exports," *New York Times,* 24 January 1992, A3. Despite the fact that many U.S. commentators and politicians have singled out Germany for criticism with respect to dual-use technology exports, such criticism might overlook or ignore America's responsibility:

> One interesting question that remains unanswered is why United States law enforcement officers have not arrested or charged many companies with violations of US export control laws related to Iraq. Other governments, such as Germany, have announced efforts to pursue dozens of companies, many very prominent, for criminal violations of export control laws. I challenge you to name one United States company that has been indicted for violating the export control laws to Iraq. (Remarks by Gonzalez, 25 April 1991, *Congressional Record,* H2547–H2557.)

One obvious answer to Gonzalez's legitimate question is that U.S. dual-use exports did not violate existing laws, perhaps indicating that they were too lenient.

47. *Middle East Arms Control and Related Issues,* 21–26; and House Committee on Banking, Finance, and Urban Affairs, *Hearing on Banca Nazionale Del*

Lavoro, 161–177. Often the focus on these sources contains a certain double standard. For example, then Senator Al Gore (D-Tenn) singled out the Swiss for criticism, without mentioning the role of U.S. corporations in the same trade. "Defeating Hussein, Once and For All," *New York Times,* 26 September 1991, A27.

48. Timmerman, *The Death Lobby,* 349–352.

49. The memorandum was made public by Representative Henry Gonzalez. See Remarks by Gonzalez, 25 April 1991, *Congressional Record,* H2551–H2553. On MIMI, see Timmerman, *The Death Lobby,* 288–289.

50. House Committee on Banking, Finance and Urban Affairs, *Hearing on Banca Nazionale Del Lavoro,* 166–177.

51. "Saddam's Agents Secretly Acquire European Shares," *Financial Times,* 25 March 1991, 1. These two firms seem to be have been the basis for organizing Iraq's procurement network in Europe. Timmerman, *The Death Lobby,* 238.

52. *Middle East Arms Control and Related Issues,* 26.

53. Remarks by Gonzalez, 25 April 1991, *Congressional Record;* William Safire, "The Lavoro Scandal," *New York Times,* 30 November 1989, A31. For overviews of this issue, see "A Fatal Attraction," *Financial Times,* 3 May 1991, 2; "Gonzalez's Iraq Expose," *Washington Post,* 22 March 1992, A1; and David Corn, "Beltway Bandits," *The Nation,* 1 June 1992.

54. House Committee on Banking, Finance, and Urban Affairs, *Hearing on Banca Nazionale Del Lavoro,* 158–162.

55. *Nightline,* 2 May 1991.

56. *Nightline,* 2 May 1991; "Payments by UK Company Linked to Iraqi Arms Network," *Financial Times,* 25 March 1991, 4; "Murdered Rocket Scientist was Funded by BNL Branch," *Financial Times,* 10 April 1991, 7; "US Indicts Iraqi in $4bn Loans Affair," *Financial Times,* 1 March 1991, 8; "Washington Accused of Iraq Loan Cover-up," *Financial Times,* 1 February 1991, 3.

57. "BNL Routinely Sent Iraqi Loans to Atlanta Unit," *Wall Street Journal,* 21 September 1989, A14; and House Committee on Banking, Finance, and Urban Affairs, *The Role of Banca Nazionale Del Lavoro in Financing Iraq,* 10–11. The question of how much the Rome headquarters knew is at the heart of this case. U.S. prosecutors trying Christopher Drogul, the BNL Atlanta chief executive, have based their case on the premise that he acted alone and thus defrauded his superiors. But if the Rome headquarters of BNL knew of the loans, then there was no fraud and therefore no case. Moreover, knowledge of potential involvement by the bank's Italian managers in the loan scheme is what the CIA allegedly withheld from the Atlanta trial. It seems probable that the U.S. prosecutors sought to try one person on the grounds he acted alone so as to avoid opening up the foreign policy implications of the case. Originally charged with 347 indictments, Drogul at first agreed to cooperate with prosecution and to plead guilty on sixty counts only, thereby ending the possibility of a trial that could disclose more information about the issue. This led the federal judge trying the case to call for the appointment of a special prosecutor to investigate an issue he feared was being covered up. "Executive Pleads Guilty in Iraq Case," *New York Times,* 3 June 1992, 15. Since subsequent developments cast serious doubt on the premise of the case, the Justice Department requested in October 1992 that the plea agreement with Drogul be withdrawn and a trial date set. "Justice Department Role Cited in Deception on Iraq Loan Data"; "C.I.A. and Justice Feud Over Inquiry in Iraq Loan Case"; and "Review Finds Inquiry Into Iraqi Loans Was Flawed," *New York Times,* 18 October 1992, 36.

58. *Nightline,* 2 May 1991.

59. "Iraq's $5 Billion Windfall Spins Deepening Mystery," *Los Angeles Times,* 24 May 1992, A1.

60. Quoted in Remarks by Gonzalez, 9 May 1991, *Congressional Record,* H2938.

61. Quoted in "A Fatal Attraction."

62. Quoted in "A Fatal Attraction." The bank executive at the center of the BNL scandal, Christopher Drogul, has alleged that the U.S. and Italian governments, as well as some of his superiors in Rome, were all aware of his credit activities on behalf of Iraq. "Former BNL Official Says US and Italy Knew of Loans to Iraq," *Financial Times,* 1 April 1992, 6.

63. "Italian Report Suggests U.S. Knew of Bank's Loans for Iraqi Inquiry," *Los Angeles Times,* 18 April, 1992, A14.

64. "Officials Worried by BNL Missile Links," *Financial Times,* 14 March 1991, 3.

65. William Safire, "Lavoro Unfolds," *New York Times,* 25 May 1990, A27; ABC News, *Nightline,* 2 May 1991; "Saddam's Son-in-law Linked to Bank Fraud," *Financial Times,* 30 January 1991, 2; William Safire, "Obstructing Justice," *New York Times,* 9 July 1992, A21; Remarks by Gonzalez, 25 April 1991, *Congressional Record*; and "A Fatal Attraction."

66. "Bush Aides' Ethics Questioned Over Loans to Iraq," *Washington Post,* 29 April 1992, A6; and Remarks by Gonzalez, 25 April 1991, *Congressional Record,* H2549–H2552.

67. "Kissinger's Firm Linked to BNL," *Financial Times,* 26 April 1991, 20; CBS News, *60 Minutes,* 29 March 1992.

68. Joe Conason, "The Iraq Lobby: Kissinger, the Business Forum & Co.," in *The Gulf War Reader,* ed. Sifry and Cerf.

69. "Bush Nominee Defended Probe Target," *Washington Post,* 9 May 1992, A10; "U.S. Attorney Role Raised in Iraq Case," *New York Times,* 24 May 1992, 15.

70. "The President's News Conference With Regional Reporters, 18 December 1990," *Weekly Compilation,* 2051. It is indicative of media coverage of the conflict that this question came from a regional reporter rather than from the White House press corps.

71. Quoted on *Nightline,* 28 October 1992.

72. House Committee on Foreign Affairs, *The Persian Gulf Crisis,* 1. Emphasis added.

73. All these terms are found in a single paragraph from one writer. Johnson, "The Just War Tradition and the American Military," 22.

74. "In Defense of Saudi Arabia (Speech of August 8, 1990)," in *The Gulf War Reader,* ed. Sifry and Cerf, 197.

75. Schuler, "Congress Must Take a Hard Look at Iraq's Charges Against Kuwait."

76. Tetreault, "Autonomy, Necessity, and the Small State," 584.

77. Springborg, "Origins of the Gulf Crisis," 230.

78. Cooley, "Pre-War Gulf Diplomacy," 26.

79. Schuler, "Congress Must Take a Hard Look at Iraq's Charges Against Kuwait."

80. Milton Viorst, "A Reporter at Large: The House of Hashem," *The New Yorker,* 7 January 1991, 43.

81. Cooley, "Pre-War Gulf Diplomacy," 126. For additional background on

these statements, see Simpson, *From the House of War,* 96–99; Walid Khalidi, "Iraq vs. Kuwait: Claims and Counterclaims," in *The Gulf War Reader,* ed. Sifry and Cerf; Salinger and Laurent, *Secret Dossier,* 5–11. For an interpretation of these events that is in agreement with the details but strongly critical of Iraqi policy, see Karsh and Rautsi, "Why Saddam Hussein Invaded Kuwait."

82. Cooley, "Pre-War Gulf Diplomacy," 126–127. For the text of the Iraqi grievances, see Salinger and Laurent, *Secret Dossier,* Appendix I.

83. Hermann, "The Middle East and the New World Order."

84. Emery, *How Mr. Bush Got His War,* 7, 9–10. Apparently, a leaked copy of a letter from the Saudi king to the Kuwaiti emir, speaking of an agreement, was published in some Arab newspapers. The existence and nature of the deal is confirmed by Cooley, "Pre-War Gulf Diplomacy," 128.

85. The account of Kuwaiti intransigence is in Simpson, *From the House of War,* 108. The story of Iraqi arrogance is in Bulloch and Morris, *Saddam's War,* 100–105; while Cooley, in "Pre-War Gulf Diplomacy," 128, maintains that progress on the payment of monies was made. Tetreault, in "Autonomy, Necessity, and the Small State," 587, cites Kuwaiti sources as declaring financial concessions were made and Iraqi sources as saying they weren't, while noting that media reports in the United States spoke of Kuwaiti arrogance.

86. Simpson, *From the House of War,* 106–107.

87. Salinger and Laurent, *Secret Dossier,* 75.

88. Emery, *How Mr. Bush Got His War,* 10–11; and Salinger and Laurent, *Secret Dossier,* 65.

89. Viorst, "Reporter at Large," 43.

90. Quoted in Salinger and Laurent, *Secret Dossier,* 241. The entire document is reprinted there as Appendix III.

91. Salinger and Laurent, *Secret Dossier,* 44. See also Viorst, "Reporter at Large."

92. Schuler, "Congress Must Take a Hard Look at Iraq's Charges Against Kuwait."

93. Emery, *How Mr. Bush Got His War,* 6.

94. "Gates, in Mideast, is Said to Discuss Ouster of Hussein," *New York Times,* 7 February 1992, A1. The possibility of a provocation through the inspection regime became most obvious in August 1992 when reports of a planned military strike began to circulate. See "U.S. Said to Plan Raids on Baghdad Over Inspections," *New York Times,* 16 August 1992, A1.

95. Anderson and Rashidian, *Iraq and the Continuing Middle East Crisis,* 108; Cooley, "Pre-War Gulf Diplomacy," 126–128.

96. Springborg, "The Origins of the Gulf War," 229. The latter two developments brought opposition from other elements in the U.S. administration dedicated to keeping ties with Iraq open.

97. "Washington's Covert Role in Saddam Oil Plot," *The Observer,* 21 October 1990, 1.

98. To warrant a just pre-emptive strike, Walzer argues that a sufficient threat has to exist. In his words, such a threat must satisfy three criteria: "a manifest intent to injure, a degree of active preparation that makes the intent a positive danger, and a general situation in which waiting, or doing anything other than fighting, greatly magnifies the risk." Walzer, *Just and Unjust Wars,* 81.

99. Walzer, *Just and Unjust Wars,* 85.

100. Johnson, "The Just War Tradition and the American Military," 22–23.

4

Washed in Shades of Gray II

Prewar Possibilities

The congressional resolution authorizing the use of military force in the Gulf depended on two key assumptions. The first, discussed in the previous chapter, was the unprovoked aggression of Iraq. The second, a pivotal notion in the ascription of the conflict as just, was that war was a last resort. Section 2(b) of that resolution required the president to determine that "the United States has used all appropriate and other peaceful means to obtain compliance by Iraq with the United Nations Security Council Resolutions...."[1] The president met that requirement on 16 January 1991 with a letter to the Speaker of the House and the president pro-tem of the Senate, in which he simply repeated, as fact rather than contention, the resolution's wording.[2]

Although United Nations Resolution 660 called on Iraq and Kuwait "to begin immediately intensive negotiations for the resolution of their differences," and expressed "support" for "all efforts in this regard,"[3] U.S. diplomacy in this crisis had little concern for anything other than the marshalling of multilateral support for military action by the United States. As one observer noted, "As for diplomacy, Washington never did see a role for it in settling the Gulf crisis."[4] After the president decided that the goal of the United States was to restore the status quo ante in Kuwait—a decision that General Colin Powell allegedly heard of by watching CNN[5]—there was little if any public discussion about the possibility for a negotiated solution to the invasion. On the contrary, various spokespersons for the administration continually emphasized that nothing should be done that could be taken to be a reward for aggression, thereby leaving little room for a nonmilitary solution. Indeed, in accounts of decisionmaking in the early days of the crisis, the option of diplomacy is remarkably conspicuous by its absence.[6]

Accordingly, when President Bush announced at the end of November 1990 that he was sending the secretary of state to Baghdad (subsequent to the doubling of U.S. military forces in the Gulf and the passage of United Nations Resolution 678 authorizing "all means necessary" to achieve the liberation of Kuwait), the trip's purpose was, as he pointedly described it, to conduct "discussions" rather than "negotiations." Indeed, when Secretary Baker finally met Iraqi Foreign Minister Tariq Aziz in Geneva on 9 January 1991, he declared that his purpose had been "not to negotiate . . . but . . . to communicate."[7] Few media outlets sought to challenge this approach as an appropriate strategy. On the eve of the war, *The Times* of London declared, "Blame for the failure of diplomacy since August 2 lies squarely with Iraq. Now, the only choice lies between capitulation to evil or a fight."[8] Likewise, after the war, *Time* relegated diplomacy to this observation: "Saddam also issued a flurry of offers to negotiate, but his antics seemed intended mainly to avert a military showdown."[9]

Although U.S. diplomacy was in the end "limited to delivery of an ultimatum: capitulate or die,"[10] there were moments, nonetheless, in which senior officials, intentionally or otherwise, left the impression that a nonmilitary solution was possible. Even President Bush's October 1990 address to the United Nations General Assembly was more flexible than subsequent newspaper reports acknowledged.[11] When the address was interpreted, however, as compatible with the earlier peace proposal of French President Mitterrand—in which an Iraqi withdrawal was linked with an international conference on the Arab-Israeli conflict—the White House moved quickly to distance itself from a positive interpretation.[12] Nevertheless, it was Secretary of State Baker who had been most interested in a negotiated solution. One report indicates that U.S. Ambassador to the UN Thomas Pickering sketched out in August 1990 a five-point plan, later endorsed by Baker, to be communicated to Iraq through Jordan. Whether or not it reached President Hussein remains uncertain, but the plan seems to have held the possibility of renegotiating the very issues that had been contested between Iraq and Kuwait at the Jeddah meeting in July 1990.[13]

Of course, judging Iraqi intentions remains a difficult proposition. As shall be shown later in this chapter, there is evidence that the Iraqi regime undertook a number of peace initiatives that were ignored by the United States and its allies. Aside from this, however, one observer points to an interesting piece of evidence indicating that permanent occupation of Kuwait was not Iraq's goal. After the invasion of Kuwait and its subsequent annexation as the nineteenth province of "Saddamiyat Mitla," Iraq issued maps in which the bulk of Kuwait appeared as that province, but in which the island of Bubiyan, the oilfield of Rumaila, and a strip of borderland called Mitla constituted part of the already existing Iraqi province of Basra, thereby suggesting that those areas were, in accordance with its preinvasion claims, Iraq's primary concern.[14]

Whatever Iraq's intentions, for those who maintained that the conflict satisfied all the criteria of just-war theory, including the criterion that war be a last resort, taken up only after exploring all other reasonable alternatives, the record of U.S. diplomacy did not pose a problem. Arguing that opponents of the war were using the criterion of "last resort" as "virtually an arithmetic concept"—by which it could always be insisted that just one more diplomatic initiative might offer the solution—many just-war theorists pronounced themselves satisfied with the diplomatic efforts of the United States.[15]

Nonetheless, there is sufficient evidence to support the view that there were other diplomatic possibilities for the resolution of the crisis. Attached to the president's brief letter to Congress of 16 January 1991 was the executive's *Report for Use in Connection with Section 2(b) of the Joint Congressional Resolution Authorizing the Use of Military Force Against Iraq.* While it was meant to be a summary of all the means followed to secure a peaceful resolution to the crisis, it began with a revealing qualification: "It is not a definitive rendition of these means, because the Administration cannot, of necessity, include at this time all the factual data that would support a complete historical record."[16] Indeed, far from being a comprehensive attempt to convey the richness of the historical record for the period prior to the 15 January deadline for an Iraqi withdrawal, the report contented itself with an account of multilateral diplomacy at the United Nations. Other sources indicate, however, that had the U.S. administration demonstrated willingness to explore negotiated options, a diplomatic resolution might well have been achieved. Given the patchy nature of the public record surrounding this issue and the inherent uncertainties of diplomacy, my purpose is not to make the case that a diplomatic solution was likely, but only to render problematic the conviction that it was impossible.[17]

The first diplomatic effort for a resolution came from members of the Arab League in the days immediately following the Iraqi invasion of Kuwait.[18] In particular, Jordan's King Hussein had shuttled between Baghdad, Riyadh, and Cairo in an attempt to convene a minisummit on 5 August. Iraq is said to have wanted this meeting to be a forum in which the Kuwaitis and Saudis could be persuaded to accept the agreement blocked at the preinvasion Jeddah summit.[19] In a transcript of the Baghdad meeting between President Hussein and UN Secretary-General Perez de Cuellar held on 13 January 1991—released by the Iraqis but confirmed by the UN as accurate in its contents—Hussein is recorded as declaring:

> We agreed to the convening of a summit conference in Saudi Arabia to be attended by five countries—Iraq, Yemen, Jordan, Saudi Arabia and

Egypt. We wanted to discuss all these complications within the Arab hemisphere and resolve them. But what happened? Instead of convening the five-state conference, it was cancelled by Saudi Arabia and Egypt and they agreed with the US to deploy its forces in Saudi territory. Thus we lost the opportunity for an Arab solution.[20]

President Hussein had apparently agreed to attend the proposed minisummit as long as his military action was not immediately and publicly condemned by the Arab League. Whether or not his condition was reasonable, it could not be met in any case once Egypt—although aware of the condition—released a statement denouncing the invasion. The Jordanians considered this action to be antithetical to Egypt's own assurances of support for King Hussein's diplomatic efforts. Most importantly, the denunciation was thought by a number of sources to be a response to extensive U.S. pressure placed upon the Egyptians to make a public stand alongside the United States.[21]

The Decision to Deploy

The U.S. decision to send military forces to Saudi Arabia, beginning with the 82nd Airborne Regiment, was part of the pressure applied to Arab allies that resulted in the curtailment of diplomatic possibilities. Those forces were deployed on the assumption that Saudi Arabia was vulnerable to Iraqi attack (a notion that had been the subject of a U.S. Central Command war game called Internal Look in July 1990),[22] and had requested them. It seems, however, that the Saudis "asked for the help the Americans were determined to give."[23] Although Saudi border scouts found no evidence of advancing Iraqis during their forays across the Kuwaiti frontier, in the absence of an independent intelligence capability, the Saudis were forced to rely on U.S. intelligence, which interpreted its data as demonstrating that Iraqi forces were massing in the south of Kuwait and threatening the kingdom.[24] Indeed, had the Saudis been equipped with their own intelligence sources, they may have seen a completely different picture. Soviet satellite photographs taken on 11 September and 13 September 1990 disclosed no evidence of a massive Iraqi build-up in Kuwait, while the Bush administration claimed there were 360,000 Iraqi troops and 2,800 Iraqi tanks in the area at that time. Reviewed by U.S. analysts with considerable experience in photographic interpretation, these photos offered no evidence of the infrastructure, fortifications, or movements required of the substantial force the United States claimed was occupying Kuwait.

One of the analysts had worked for the Arms Control and Disarmament Agency in the Reagan administration, and the other had been employed by the Defense Intelligence Agency; neither found any evidence for the presence of an Iraqi force even 20 percent as large as the one the administration claimed was in place, even though U.S. forces in Saudi Arabia were clearly visible. They observed no Iraqi tent cities for troops, no tank congregations, and no Iraqi planes at a deserted Kuwaiti air force base—all this five weeks after the invasion. Nor could they observe any of the infrastructure such as water supplies required to service troops. Likewise, there was no visible evidence of movement. While the analysts could see the tire tracks of civilian vehicles that serviced the oil fields, they could see no tank tracks or any other marks that would have been left by the troops and tanks the Pentagon declared were there. Indeed, Kuwaiti roads leading to the Saudi border— unlike those in Saudi Arabia—had sand deposits blown across them, indicating they were impassable by trucks and weren't being kept clear by the Iraqi military. The analysts dismissed the possibility that troops were there but hidden or invisible to the satellite and did not accept that the photos were disinformation, arguing that Soviet prospects for making money from future sales of this data would have been hurt were the information false or misleading. In conclusion, the analysts argued that the occupation of Kuwait City might have been accomplished by a force of only ten thousand soldiers. No one doubts, however, that by January 1991 Iraqi forces in and around Kuwait were much larger, though this story leaves open the possibility that (a) the original invasion was intended to achieve an aim other than occupation and annexation; and (b) the Iraqis responded to the U.S. build-up, rather than the other way around.

Interestingly, the U.S. media attributed little importance to the Soviet photographs. Although ABC purchased the satellite photos for $1,560 in November 1990, it declined to run a story based upon them because it did not have an image that covered southern Kuwait. Why the network did not purchase such a photo is not clear. When a Florida newspaper, the *St. Petersburg Times,* purchased the additional photographs, including one of Saudi Arabia, it retained the two analysts who offered the above interpretation. Prior to publication of the story, the Pentagon declined to explain the discrepancy between the photographs and its own version of events. After publication, the national wire services declined to transmit the story, and no other major newspapers followed up on it.[25]

Even if these photos were false or incorrectly interpreted, there is little doubt that the United States massively overestimated the size of the Iraqi army in and around Kuwait. It now appears that the publicly cited figure, over five hundred thousand troops, was actually between two and three times the correct number. The United States probably derived the figure of 540,000 Iraqi troops by assuming that the thirty-eight Iraqi divisions were at or near full strength (fifteen thousand troops).[26] Whether a deliberate inflation or an inadvertent calculation, this intelligence failure could have resulted in a significant misreading of Iraqi capabilities and intentions, thereby restricting the space for diplomacy. Moreover, it reflected precisely the same flawed logic that produced inflated threat assessments of the Soviets in the early days of the Cold War.[27] More recent military estimates have calculated the number of Iraqi troops at 350,000 by the start of the air war, with that reduced to 183,000 by the start of the ground war.[28]

Iraqi Proposals

Throughout the crisis, there were a number of diplomatic proposals passed from Iraq to the United States. On or about 10 August 1990 two Arab-American businessmen friendly with White House Chief of Staff John Sununu presented a message from the Iraqi deputy foreign minister, proposing the withdrawal of all troops in return for guaranteed Iraqi access to the Gulf, Iraqi control of the Rumaila oil field, and discussions between Iraq and the United States on oil prices. Although the response from Sununu and national security advisor Scowcroft was noncommittal, the offer was not ruled out of hand. When resistance to the initiative was conveyed to Baghdad, the terms of the offer were broadened to include the release of all foreign hostages, with this revised version of the plan reportedly presented to the United States on 23 August. On two occasions in the subsequent week, officials at the Iraqi Foreign Ministry in Baghdad inquired with their embassy in Washington to see if the message had been delivered and whether or not any response was forthcoming. The United States did not respond, and the initiative died. According to a confidential congressional report of these events, they demonstrated that "a diplomatic solution satisfactory to the interests of the United States may well have been possible since the earliest days of the invasion."[29]

Elements of this proposal were made public by Iraq on 12 August; the Iraqis were later said to have been incensed that the United States didn't follow the diplomatic protocol of requesting an official transcript of the initiative's public announcement.[30] The proposal was quickly dismissed by the United States, which rejected any plan that sought to link various conflicts in the Middle East. Some commentators nonetheless thought it was not without merit.[31] President Hussein, ruminating upon the proposal's reception in his meeting with UN Secretary-General Perez de Cuellar, reflected, "On 12 August we made an initiative. We did not think that it would be accepted in full. However, we never thought that it would be turned down without being looked into. The President of the US turned down the initiative while he was on the plane two hours after it was announced without looking into it."[32] Finally, an additional Iraqi plan playing down any linkage with the Palestinian issue was presented to the United States through Yugoslavian emissaries on 2 January 1991. As was the case with the 23 August initiative, some U.S. officials outside of the inner core of decisionmakers characterized it as "serious" and "negotiable,"[33] but nothing came of it.

Representatives of other countries made forays into the diplomatic netherland to see if a solution could be brokered. French officials were prominent in this regard, but one of the most promising missions came from Soviet President Gorbachev's envoy, Yevgeny Primakov. In the first week of October 1990 he traveled between Baghdad, Moscow, and London; but despite hearing some small but encouraging noises from the Iraqis, he encountered nothing but stiff opposition from British Prime Minister Thatcher, who, he thought, had made up her mind to break the back of Iraq's military and industrial capacity.[34] At the same time, Saudi Arabian officials were hinting at the possibility of a negotiated settlement through territorial compromise, but U.S. officials quickly put an end to the speculation the hints engendered.[35] In addition, Primakov himself tried to prevent a ground war through negotiations with the Iraqis in late February 1991. Although he successfully obtained their agreement to an unconditional withdrawal from Kuwait, his efforts were rejected by the United States and its allies, who wanted to press on with the military conflict. As one of Schwarzkopf's officers observed, "The Soviets [were] talking about getting us exactly what we asked for, and we summarily turned them down."[36] Had Primakov's work been accepted, tens of thousands of Iraqis and a not insignificant number of coalition forces would have been saved from death.

The final diplomatic initiative of note was launched by Algerian President Benjedid in early December 1990. With a formidable reputation as the Arab world's most respected mediator—he had, for example, successfully aided the United States in its negotiations with Iran over the embassy hostages—he initiated his mission through talks with an envoy of the Saudis' King Fahd. Nonetheless, Benjedid's mission—which included plans for an Iraqi-Saudi summit after an Iraqi promise to withdraw from Kuwait—failed shortly after it began, when both the United States and Saudi Arabia refused to meet with him in person. During a stopover in Amman, Jordan, Benjedid was informed through European channels that the United States had officially asked the Saudis not to receive him.[37] Most importantly, the fate of the Benjedid initiative indicates that it was not only by omission that the United States declined to pursue a diplomatic solution to the Gulf crisis. By commission—by direct interventions to thwart a number of possible Arab solutions—the United States sought to make a military option the only option. In consequence, it is at best disingenuous for those reiterating the dominant narrative of the war to protest that the infinite possibilities of diplomacy and the criterion of "last resort" merely delay war, given a concerted effort either to avoid or to scuttle negotiations from the outset.

POINTING THE FINGER

In the social and political drama of the Gulf crisis, the discourse on moral certitude relied considerably upon the subject of human rights to accrue moral capital for the United States and its allies. Indeed, because it was maintained that, in Brigadier General Glosson's words, "there were no worse people on the face of the earth" than the Iraqi military,[38] a number of those who fought in or supported the war felt that the United States and its allies were uninhibited by histories such as those assembled above and therefore permitted to act without restraint. Accounts of Iraqi human rights abuses were thus pivotal to the rite of passage in this crisis.[39]

When Amnesty International released a report in December 1990 on human rights abuses in Kuwait during the Iraqi occupation, it was hastily adopted by administration spokespersons as grist for their mill.[40] In stark contrast to Amnesty's measured tone and lack of moral posturing, leaders from the president on down took the report to be unassailable proof for their established and loudly declared convictions. For example, the report was the backdrop for Bush's remark in the David Frost interview that the crisis we faced had the greatest moral importance of any since World War II, for his January 1991 letter to college campuses, in which he asserted that the issue was "black and white," and for his talks with congressional leaders on 3 January.[41] Likewise, stories cited in the report were used to motivate U.S. troops prior to the ground war. One U.S. army captain revealed that soldiers were given briefings every night on the atrocities Iraq had committed in Kuwait, "so every time we got out there, there was no holding back so Saddam can't do this again."[42] While the army troops were briefed in this fashion to pump them up for combat, U.S. navy fliers aboard the carrier USS *Kennedy* watched pornographic movies for motivation before a mission. Among many other details of daily military conduct, this information was deleted from a media pool report by military censors.[43]

To be sure, Amnesty's December 1990 report detailed many human rights abuses by Iraqi forces in Kuwait worthy of strong condemnation. As the Amnesty report noted, however, these were not developments novel to the occupation of Kuwait:

> These violations which have been reported since 2 August are entirely consistent with abuses known to have been committed in Iraq over many

years, and which have been documented by Amnesty International in its numerous reports. . . . Amnesty International has repeatedly placed such information on the public record, and regrets that until the invasion of Kuwait, the international community did not see fit to apply serious pressure in an attempt to put an end to these abuses.[44]

Amnesty International was so incensed by the administration's selective use of its material that it released a statement in which the organization's executive director criticized the administration for remaining "mute" to accounts of Iraqi human rights abuses prior to August 1990.[45] Unlike the allegations contained in the report, this statement was largely ignored by the media. Amnesty repeated its concerns at a January 1991 congressional hearing on Iraqi human rights abuses, where the director argued that a recipient of the Nobel Peace Prize should not be employed to beat the drum of war.[46]

Amnesty was supported by other major human rights groups. In February 1990 Middle East Watch had issued a lengthy report on Iraqi abuses and called for sanctions. Media outlets loud in their denunciations of Iraq after 2 August were then conspicuously silent.[47] Citing a record of mistreatment and abuses, Middle East Watch argued that

except in the matter of Iraq's use of chemical weapons—and even then with little consistency—the Reagan and Bush administrations have paid scant attention to human rights in their dealings with Iraq. Both have put the nurturing of newly friendly relations with President Saddam Hussein well ahead of addressing the violent and repressive nature of his regime.[48]

Not only did the Bush administration fail to respond at that time, it was actively lobbying Congress to head off any moves to impose sanctions. Moreover, in the year following the reported use of Iraqi chemical weapons against Kurdish villages—a crime later cited incessantly by the administration as proof of Iraq's deplorable human rights record—the Bush administration doubled the value of agricultural credits available to Iraq and stalled an initiative to have the United Nations Human Rights Commission investigate the situation there.[49] Though some reports question the exact circumstances in which chemical weapons were used against the Kurdish village of Halabja, where five thousand people reportedly died, there is little doubt that there has been an extensive and organized campaign of violent repression (if not attempted genocide) involving chemical weapons against the Kurds by the Iraqis.[50]

One detail among many in the Amnesty report of December 1990 ignited particular interest in the Bush administration.[51] Toward the end, and without any fanfare, the Amnesty report quoted sources who revealed that over three hundred premature babies had died since the Iraqi invasion, many of them removed by troops from their incubators. Tracing the production of this information provides insight into the intertextual quality of the process by which moral capital is accumulated.

The only eyewitness account of this allegation came from an unidentified fifteen-year-old Kuwaiti girl who had anonymously testified to the Congressional Human Rights Caucus on 10 October 1990; Amnesty acknowledged that source in its report. Now authorized with the organization's imprimatur, the allegation entered public discourse and legitimated earlier occasions in which the charge had been aired (such as when Bush spoke of "newborn babies thrown off incubators" in Dallas on 15 October 1990).[52] When the director of Amnesty testified to Congress on 8 January 1991, the report containing the charge, *Iraq/Occupied Kuwait*, was published in full as an appendix to the congressional report, thereby giving it a further audience and increased legitimation.

Once the war was over, however, it was discovered that the charge was false. Further investigations in April 1991 by Amnesty revealed that there was no evidence that any babies had been deliberately removed from incubators, and that those premature babies who had died in Kuwait did so because they failed to receive necessary care after medical personnel fled the country.[53] Moreover, it was revealed much later that the anonymous eyewitness from whose account the story received its authority was in actuality the teenage daughter of the Kuwaiti ambassador to the United States.[54] Furthermore, her testimony was part of a multimillion-dollar public relations campaign that the Kuwaiti government-in-exile had contracted the firm of Hill and Knowlton to conduct. Among that campaign's major events were the October 1990 congressional testimony and a presentation to the UN Security Council—complete with gruesome photographs and purported eyewitness accounts—just prior to its November 1990 vote authorizing the use of "all means necessary" to liberate Kuwait.[55] Although in the former instance at least some congressional representatives knew the girl's identity and the sponsors of her testimony, they said nothing at the time, thereby contributing to the generation of this powerful charge against Iraq.[56] The revelation of this produced a response from the public relations executive involved, and an angry charge from the congressman who chaired the October hearing that it was part of "revisionist" attempts to alter history.[57] In a development indicating the importance attributed to the original charge, the U.S. embassy in Kuwait was still marshalling evidence in support of its claims one year after the conflict.[58]

Both prewar chronologies and postwar events revealed that the moralism of the United States about the horrors of human rights abuses did not derive solely from an abhorrence of the practices it highlighted. Indeed, its reaction to the predicament of Kurdish refugees fleeing the civil war in Iraq demonstrated how the discourse of moral certitude functioned as a practice that bolstered the principle of sovereignty. Having encouraged (through covert operations and public declarations) a postwar rebellion inside Iraq, the Bush administration initially declined to offer official assistance for Kurds escaping the fighting, declaring that a respect for state sovereignty meant that it could not intervene in a domestic situation. However, once the number of refugees reached the hundreds of thousands, and European allies proposed the establishment of safe havens in northern Iraq, the United States decided reluctantly to act.[59] In partnership with Britain, France, and Turkey, and consistent with the idea that sovereignty refers equally to issues of authority and power, a relationship of suzerainty (in which one sovereign authority controls an autonomous region in the territory of another) was undertaken, such that the area north of the thirty-sixth parallel in Iraq was declared off limits to Saddam Hussein's military.[60]

U.S. reluctance to assist the Kurds is consistent with the ambivalence of its past policies. In the early 1970s, at the Shah of Iran's behest, the United States provided the Kurds with limited supplies so as to encourage an insurrection against the Iraqi leadership, thereby providing Iran leverage in a border dispute between the two states. Once the dispute was resolved, however, support for the Kurds was halted.[61] The involvement of Turkey in this operation was likewise not a consequence of wholly noble intentions. With a restive Kurdish population in Turkey (whom the government there derisively calls "mountain Turks"), Turkey has a strong interest in keeping the Kurds inside Iraq. Moreover, Turkey has a record of human rights abuses against this group.[62] In addition—in incidents given little prominence even though the administration continued to assail Iraq for its treatment of the Kurds—Turkey conducted during the second half of 1991 a number of military operations against Kurdish forces in northern Iraq.[63]

Furthermore, the revelation of Kuwaiti human rights abuses in the period after liberation attracted little if any criticism from the Bush administration. Instances of violent harassment, torture, unlawful detention and killing, and legal proceedings without due process have all been widely documented and linked to Kuwaiti authorities.[64] The abuses have been largely directed against Palestinians and other foreign nationals, many of whom have been accused, with little or no evidence, of collaborating with Iraq during the occupation. The Kuwaiti crown prince has described the process as "the purification of evil elements in this country."[65] Moreover, the United States is directly involved in this pattern of conduct, given that U.S. civilian affairs officers from the Pentagon are responsible for maintaining public security and justice until Kuwait is rehabilitated. Indeed, testimony provided both to the International Red Cross and to Middle East Watch has placed U.S. officers at the scene of illegal detentions and torture.[66] Instead of rebuking such practices, however, in terms consistent with the criticism of Iraq, President Bush effectively condoned them. Speaking at a news conference on 1 July 1991, he declared, "The war wasn't fought about democracy in Kuwait. The war was fought about aggression against Kuwait . . . I think we're expecting a little much if we're asking people in Kuwait to take kindly to those that had spied on their countrymen . . . and things of that nature."[67]

AT WAR

Counting the Dead

There are two domains of focus in just-war theory: whether it is just to resort to war (*jus ad bellum*), and whether there is just conduct of war (*jus in bello*). Up until this point, my argument has been concerned with episodes that unsettle any assurance about the former. In this section, I want to examine details relevant to the latter, for one of the most often made arguments in defense of the war with Iraq is the proposition that this was a conflict conducted in accordance with the principles of discrimination and proportionality.

Contrary to the videographic image of (in General Colin Powell's words) a "clean win,"[68] this was a war in which large numbers of people died. It is an obvious point, but the death-free representation of the war (actively cultivated by the Pentagon and implicitly accepted by the media) requires active contestation. This is a task made difficult by the military's aversion to any definitive assessment of Iraqi casualties.[69] Since the military used bulldozers to bury thousands of Iraqi dead in mass graves, in addition to using bulldozers to bury Iraqi troops alive as the ground war began,[70] it is more than likely that some sort of assessment has been made. Not to have done so would mean that the United States contravened the Geneva Convention's requirement that belligerents search for the dead, record information that might aid in identification, and establish their cause of death.[71] Indeed, coalition forces did provide an accounting of Iraqi casualties to the International Committee of the Red Cross at the end of March 1991, but these details were withheld from public release.[72] Perhaps they judged the public mood correctly: in England following the ceasefire in the ground war, there was a storm of protest when a major daily newspaper printed a graphic photograph of a charred Iraqi soldier; many readers argued that its publication constituted propaganda.[73]

What information is available, however, demonstrates that the war resulted in an unprecedented level of death, given its short duration. Greenpeace, which has made the most sustained analysis of casualty figures, estimates that a total of between 177,500 and 243,000 Iraqis were killed during the air war, the ground war, and the aftermath of the war. Some 70,000 to 115,000 of those people were in the military, while between 72,500 and 93,000 were civilians.[74] Greenpeace also estimates 5,000 military deaths and 30,000 civilian deaths in the civil war that erupted in Iraq after the ceasefire.

Other estimates vary wildly and depend, among other factors, upon the disparate assumptions made about the size of Iraqi forces in southern Iraq and Kuwait during the war. The only official statement released by the U.S. military tentatively estimated 100,000 Iraqi military deaths, a figure reportedly subject to a margin of error of 50 percent.[75] In other accounts, U.S. military officials offered estimates ranging from 25,000 to 200,000 military deaths.[76] The bipartisan congressional report—which argued that the size of the Iraqi army was vastly overestimated—maintained that 9,000 Iraqi troops were killed in the air war, while 120,000 escaped or were killed in the ground war.[77]

Although official U.S. military sources have made no estimate of civilian deaths, a Census Bureau analyst calculated that approximately 13,000 civilians died during the war, and that over 150,000 civilian and military deaths resulted in total from the war, the postwar rebellions, and disease and deprivation. In an episode revealing the politicized nature of the production of this knowledge, the analyst in question was subsequently dismissed for making the number public, while the bureau issued a report lowering the figure of 13,000 to 5,000. Once the analyst's dismissal became a public legal issue, the Census Bureau retracted her firing.[78] Meanwhile, other nongovernmental sources have claimed civilian casualties during the war that ranged from 11,000 to 24,000.[79]

Just as telling as the scale of death is the timing of death. According to Greenpeace, "only" 3,000 of the civilian deaths occurred during the air war, the remainder being a consequence (in the "postwar" period of March to December 1991) of the damage inflicted upon the civilian infrastructure of Iraq. This sequence of events not only challenges the fragile distinction between civilian and military targets—upon which the Pentagon placed so much emphasis—but also renders questionable the notion that a war ends when the fighting stops. Greenpeace's estimate is supported by the Middle East Watch report entitled "Needless Deaths." In addition, Middle East Watch concludes that the attacks against civilian infrastructure, including electricity, water, and sewerage facilities, contravened the 1977 Protocol 1 of the 1949 Geneva Accords.[80]

In contrast to the timing of civilian deaths, as many—and perhaps more—military deaths were inflicted during the 100-hour ground war as during the 1,000-hour air war. Indeed, the infamous "turkey shoot" of Iraqi forces at Mutla Ridge and on other highways to the north of Kuwait

City resulted in as many as 25,000 military deaths.[81] The roads were jammed with thousands of vehicles, both civilian and military, including tanks whose open hatches and waving white flags were visible to navy pilots. Nonetheless, U.S. commanders determined that this was a retreat rather than a withdrawal—even though they had systematically destroyed all means by which a withdrawal command could have been communicated to Iraqi troops—and ordered an air assault that consisted of 660 combat missions in which all aircraft, including B-52s with cluster bombs, were to use any available ordnance.[82] U.S. military officers felt that the Iraqi looting of Kuwait City justified whatever destruction coalition forces might inflict on the Iraqis as they headed home. Chief of the U.S. air staff Brigadier General Buster Glosson declared, "If I could have killed every Iraqi in Kuwait City, I would have . . . I went after that convoy primarily because of the barbaric and ruthless way they had treated people in Kuwait. There were no worse people on the face of the earth." Major General Royal Moore, the marine commander in charge of the operation, said it "was really kind of an execution" that stood as "our crowning glory."[83]

In addition to the relatively light level of coalition military casualties—far lighter, in fact, than the Pentagon expected, given that they ordered 16,099 body bags (renamed "Human Remains Pouches")[84]—in another domain as well, there were substantially fewer casualties than predicted. Planners had estimated that there could be 40,000 Kuwaiti civilians killed and another 100,000 injured during the liberation of their country. In the end, however, according to conventional wisdom, perhaps 2,000 Kuwaitis were killed or counted missing as a result of the Iraqi occupation and allied liberation.[85] Other estimates vary, but they range from "hundreds" recorded by Amnesty International to the 7,000 alleged by members of the Kuwaiti resistance. It is worth noting that this range roughly parallels the number of civilian deaths that resulted from the U.S. invasion of Panama in December 1989.[86]

Bombing Iraq

Just as the videographic representation of the war obscured the high number of casualties, it also obfuscated the nature of the bombing of Iraq. While the military fed the media a steady diet of videos depicting successful precision-guided bombing raids, it was disclosed after the war—and inadvertently at that—that the much heralded "smart" weapons constituted only 7 percent of the tonnage dropped on targets in Iraq. Some 93 percent of the total consisted of unguided "dumb" weapons, three-quarters of which missed their targets.[87] While television viewers were spellbound by the sight of Stealth aircraft sneaking up on targets, a small number of B-52s were dropping one-third of all the tonnage, in raids so intense that Royal Navy frogmen could feel the Gulf sea bed shudder.[88]

Yet, in one of the great paradoxes of the war—which challenges our received understanding of the nature of modern air warfare—the small number of "smart" bombs (20 percent of which missed their targets)[89] wrought far greater damage upon Iraqi society than the inordinately larger quantity of inaccurate weapons dropped. As one reviewer noted, "The worst civilian suffering, senior officers say, has resulted not from bombs that went astray but from precision-guided weapons that hit exactly where they were aimed—at electrical plants, oil refineries and transportation networks."[90] Thus, while the Pentagon's much-vaunted policy of avoiding civilian casualties was carried out insofar as neighborhoods were not targeted for their own sake, the actual consequences of precision-guided bombing contradicted the policy (as the postwar casualty figures cited above disclose). In something of a double irony, while smart weapons were thought to herald the possibility of new wartime strategies, it seems that they were employed in the service of war aims that sought to disable Iraqi society at large, in much the same manner as dictated by older notions of strategic bombing. That the destruction of Iraqi infrastructure was a war aim is evident in the fact that long after Iraqi troops were isolated in the south, targets such as bridges were being hit in the north. Indeed, Baghdad was subject to some of the most intense bombing of the war during the final ground phase.[91] Moreover, many of the sites on the ever expanding target list compiled by U.S. commanders were chosen because of their psychological impact or because the need for foreign assistance in order to rebuild them would generate greater postwar leverage for the allied nations. Whatever the reason, the damage to Iraq's infrastructure—which a United Nations report termed "near apocalyptic"[92]—is likely to cost more than $30 billion to repair.[93]

Other Concerns

Aside from the extent of the killing and damage inflicted upon Iraq, numerous other events and factors serve to unsettle the moral certitude surrounding the coalition's prosecution of the Gulf War:

1. The bombing of the Amiriya bunker in Baghdad (which directly killed hundreds of civilians) turned out to be neither a mistake nor the result of an intelligence failure; it was targeted as a place where the leadership might be. Indeed, a specially designed penetrating weapon was used in late February against similar bunkers in Baghdad.[94]

2. A nuclear facility was first targeted with a massive "dumb" bomb raid, contrary to assertions that only "smart" weapons were being used against such targets. Moreover, these attacks—regardless of the weapon—

were contrary to the international consensus if not the Geneva Protocols against targeting sites containing dangerous substances.[95]

3. Much was made of Iraq's potential for using chemical weapons, yet it was U.S. forces who employed during the war the closest thing to (if not actually) a chemical weapon when they used napalm against Iraqi troops and emplacements in Kuwait.[96]

4. While President Bush accused Iraq of "environmental terrorism" for setting off an oil spill in the Gulf, it turned out that about one-third of that spill resulted from allied bombing of oil facilities in southern Iraq and Kuwait. Moreover, the United States (like Iraq) refuses to abide by the specific environmental protections established in the 1977 Geneva Protocols.[97]

These paradoxes, contradictions, and reversals put into question the moral certitude of the political discourse framing the conflict. In particular, they challenge the declaration of one triumphalist postwar publication, which argued that because "Saddam Hussein [was] so cartoon-villainous (and so incompetent as a military leader), [and] that his soldiers . . . committed atrocities . . . [it] took the moral onus off the carnage that the coalition left in its wake."[98] Nonetheless, many will complain that in the "fog of war" the normally troubling disjuncture between moral standards and combat performance has to be set aside as an unfortunate by-product of the situation. Their argument might carry some weight were it not for the fact that this war was presented and sold on unabashedly ethical grounds that resonated with the just-war notions of discrimination and proportionality. In consequence, the account rendered here does no more than apply the standards established by the United States and its allies to their prosecution of the conflict.

NOTES

1. House Committee on Foreign Affairs, *The Persian Gulf Crisis*, 1.
2. House Committee on Foreign Affairs, *The Persian Gulf Crisis*, 123.
3. Bennis and Moushabeck, *Beyond the Storm*, 376.
4. John Newhouse, "The Diplomatic Round: Misreadings," *The New Yorker*, 18 February 1991, 74.
5. Woodward, *The Commanders*, 260.
6. Woodward, *The Commanders*; and "From the First, U.S. Resolve to Fight," *New York Times*, 3 March 1991, 1.
7. Quoted in Salinger and Laurent, *Secret Dossier*, 209.
8. "No Choice But War," *The Times*, 16 January 1991, in *Despatches from the Gulf War*, ed. MacArthur, 17.
9. Quoted in Friedrich, ed., *Desert Storm*, 29.
10. Chomsky, "After the Cold War," 28–29.

11. See Elizabeth Drew, "Letter from Washington," *The New Yorker,* 15 October 1990.

12. *Facts on File,* 26 October 1990, 789. For details of the French proposal, see Lauterpacht et al., eds., *Basic Documents,* 287–288.

13. John Newhouse, "The Diplomatic Round: Building a Cage," *The New Yorker,* 8 October 1990.

14. Newhouse, "The Diplomatic Round," 106.

15. George Weigel, "War, Peace, and the Christian Conscience," in *Just War and the Gulf War,* ed. Johnson and Weigel, 60. See also Johnson, "The Just War Tradition and the American Military," 29; and Walzer, *Just and Unjust Wars,* 2d ed., xiii–xv.

16. House Committee on Foreign Affairs, *The Persian Gulf Crisis,* 124.

17. For a narrative that shares a number of common points with what follows, see Staniland, *Getting to No.* For reviews of the diplomatic possibilities and strategies, see "Reflections on the War in the Persian Gulf."

18. For the texts associated with this and other initiatives, see *Basic Documents,* Chapter 7.

19. Emery, *How Mr. Bush Got His War,* 14; Cooley, "Pre-War Gulf Diplomacy," 130; and Salinger and Laurent, *Secret Dossier,* 96–114.

20. "A Bitter Cup of Coffee in Baghdad," *The Independent,* 14 February 1991.

21. Simpson, *From the House of War,* 136–138; and Salinger and Laurent, *Secret Dossier,* 165.

22. Brown and Shukman, *All Means Necessary,* vii, 11. On the importance of war gaming and simulations to the military logic of the crisis, see Der Derian, "War Games May Prove Deadly." Schwarzkopf made an interesting observation about the reality of the simulation and the simulation of reality surrounding Internal Look:

> To make the drill more realistic, several weeks in advance I'd asked our message center to start sending a stream of fictional dispatches about military and political developments in Iraq to the headquarters of the Army, Navy, Air Force, and Marine units scheduled to participate. As the war game began, the message center also passed along routine intelligence bulletins about the *real* Middle East. Those concerning Iraq were so similar to the game dispatches that the message center ended up having to stamp the fictional reports with a prominent disclaimer: "Exercise Only." (Schwarzkopf, *It Doesn't Take a Hero,* 291.)

23. Bulloch and Morris, *Saddam's War,* 139.

24. Brown and Shukman, *All Means Necessary,* 12; Woodward, *The Commanders,* 258–259.

25. "Photos Don't Show Buildup," *St. Petersburg Times* (Florida), 6 January 1991, 1A; and Yant, *Desert Mirage,* 91.

26. Freedman and Karsh, "How Kuwait Was Won," 13.

27. See Evangelista, "Stalin's Postwar Army Reappraised"; and Garthoff, "Estimating Soviet Military Force Levels."

28. Simpson, *From the House of War,* 332; Freedman and Karsh, "How Kuwait Was Won," 13; Arkin, Durrant, and Cherni, *On Impact,* 42–43; and "Report: Allies Faced Only 183,000 Iraqis," *Washington Post,* 24 April 1992, A25.

29. Robert Parry, "The Peace Feeler That Was," *The Nation,* 15 April 1991. Elements of this are also reported in Salinger and Laurent, *Secret Dossier,* 127.

30. Milton Viorst, "Report from Baghdad," *The New Yorker,* 24 September 1990, 92.

31. While the *New York Times* dismissed it with one line of coverage, the

Financial Times of London editorialized that it was a positive development that should not be ignored.

32. "A Bitter Cup of Coffee in Baghdad," *The Independent,* 14 February 1991.

33. Steve Niva, "The Battle is Joined," in *Beyond the Storm,* ed. Bennis and Moushabeck, 58, 65; Chomsky, "After the Cold War," 28.

34. Simpson, *From the House of War,* 226–231; and Cooley, "Pre-War Gulf Diplomacy," 136. Primakov wrote a book (*The War That Need Not Have Been*) detailing his experiences, but it has not been published outside of Russia.

35. *Facts on File,* 26 October 1990, 789.

36. Quoted in Schwarzkopf, *It Doesn't Take a Hero,* 442. Concern among the leadership in Washington at the possibility of a Soviet-brokered withdrawal was conveyed to Schwarzkopf in a conversation with General Colin Powell, where the latter states: "I've got a whole bunch of people here looking at this Russian proposal and they're all upset. My President wants to get on with this thing [the ground war]. My secretary wants to get on with it. *We need to get on with this.*" Quoted in Schwarzkopf, *It Doesn't Take A Hero,* 443.

37. Jaber, "Saudi Arabia Dampens Arab Peace Bids"; Salinger and Laurent, *Secret Dossier,* 205; Cooley, "Pre-War Gulf Diplomacy," 134–135.

38. Quoted in Brown and Shukman, *All Means Necessary,* 154.

39. See Labonski and Parker, "Human Rights as Rhetoric."

40. Amnesty International, *Iraq/Occupied Kuwait.*

41. Woodward, *The Commanders,* 343, 354; and Yant, *Desert Mirage,* 53–56.

42. Quoted in Brown and Shukman, *All Means Necessary,* 149.

43. Robert Fisk, "Free to Report What We are Told," *The Independent,* 6 February 1991, 19.

44. Amnesty International, *Iraq/Occupied Kuwait,* 4. Earlier reports include *Iraq*; *Children*; and *Iraqi Kurds.*

45. Quoted in Yant, *Desert Mirage,* 54–55.

46. See House Committee on Foreign Affairs, *Hearing on Human Rights Abuses in Kuwait and Iraq.*

47. Conason, "The Iraq Lobby," in *The Gulf War Reader,* ed. Sifry and Cerf, 84.

48. Middle East Watch, *Human Rights in Iraq,* 101.

49. Middle East Watch, *Human Rights in Iraq,* 103–104, 108–109, 113–114; and "US Backed $1bn Iraqi Loan Prior to Invasion of Kuwait," *Financial Times,* 3 May 1991, 1.

50. See "Years Later, No Clear Culprit in Gassing of Kurds," *New York Times,* 28 April 1991, 13; "Iraqi Files Point to Mass Deaths," *Washington Post,* 22 February 1992, 1.

51. Amnesty International, *Iraq/Occupied Kuwait,* 5.

52. Waas, "What Washington Gave Saddam for Christmas," 95.

53. Alexander Cockburn, "Beat the Devil," *The Nation,* 13 May 1991; Brown and Shukman, *All Means Necessary,* 165–166. Amnesty's original report had noted that the majority of hospital deaths were attributable to the exodus of medical staff. See *Iraq/Occupied Kuwait,* 55.

54. John MacArthur, "Remember Nayirah, Witness for Kuwait?" *New York Times,* 6 January 1992.

55. Rowse, "Flacking for the Emir."

56. "Congressman Says Girl Was Credible," *New York Times,* 12 January 1991, 11.

57. See Thomas E. Eidson, "P.R. Firm Had No Reason to Question Kuwaiti's

Testimony," Letter to the Editor, *New York Times,* 15 January 1992; and Tom Lantos, "Kuwaiti Gave Consistent Account of Atrocities," Letter to the Editor, *New York Times,* 27 January 1992.

58. "U.S. Offers Proof of Iraqi Atrocity," *New York Times,* 6 February 1992, A11. Although this report speaks of proof, the new information amounts to an eyewitness account by anonymous sources alleging two incidents in which eight babies died. Middle East Watch maintains that while it cannot rule on isolated instances of infant deaths, it has disproved the charges of official infanticide.

59. "How Bush Overcame Reluctance and Embraced Kurdish Relief," *New York Times,* 18 April 1991, A16.

60. For the dispute over the principle of sovereignty and suzerainty with respect to the Kurds, see William Safire, "Duty to Intervene," *New York Times,* 15 April 1991, A17; Brian Urquhart, "Sovereignty vs. Suffering," *New York Times,* 17 April 1991, A23; and Chopra and Weiss, "Sovereignty is No Longer Sacrosanct."

61. Daniel Schorr, "Washington Has Betrayed the Kurds Before," *Manchester Guardian Weekly,* 14 April 1991, 18.

62. See, for example, Amnesty International, *Iraqi Kurds.*

63. "Turkey Attacks Kurds in Iraq for Second Day," *New York Times,* 28 October 1991, A3.

64. Andrew Whitley, "The Dirty War in Kuwait," *New York Times,* 2 April 1991, A19; Kenneth Roth, "Mass Graves in Kuwait," *New York Times,* 11 June 1991, A23; Aryeh Neier, "Watching Rights," *The Nation,* 23 September 1991; and "Kuwait Finds New Ways to Harass its Palestinians," *Manchester Guardian Weekly,* 19 January 1992, 14.

65. Quoted in Brown and Shukman, *All Means Necessary,* 173.

66. Whitley, "The Dirty War in Kuwait." Robert Fisk of *The Independent* witnessed the kidnapping of a Palestinian by Kuwaiti officials. When he tried to intervene, the U.S. special forces officer overseeing the incident announced to him: "This is martial law, boy. Fuck off!" Robert Fisk, "Out of the Pool," *Mother Jones,* May/June 1991, 56.

67. Quoted in Neier, "Watching Rights."

68. Quoted in Norris, "Military Censorship and the Body Count in the Persian Gulf War," 224. On the video presentation of the war, see Der Derian, "Videographic War II."

69. This antipathy is said to revolve around the desire not to repeat a practice thought to have weakened the U.S. position during the Vietnam War. But it is worth remembering that the body count in Vietnam was not an affirmation of the worth of Vietnamese lives, but a quantification of U.S. superiority devised by the military.

70. Arkin, Durrant, and Cherni, *On Impact,* 44; and "U.S. Army Buried Iraqi Soldiers Alive in Gulf War," *New York Times,* 15 September 1991, 10.

71. Holly Burkholter, "Some Bodies Don't Count," *Los Angeles Times,* 12 March 1991, B11. These are the grounds upon which the United States continues to press Vietnam for more information on the 2,300 U.S. soldiers still listed as missing in action.

72. Arkin, Durrant, and Cherni, *On Impact,* 44.

73. Harold Evans, "A Necessary Shock," *The Observer,* 17 March 1991, in *Despatches from the Gulf,* ed. MacArthur, 256–258.

74. Greenpeace, *Iraqi Deaths from the Gulf War as of December 1991.*

75. "Iraq's War Toll Estimated by U.S.," *New York Times,* 5 June 1991, A5.

76. "Military Experts See a Death Toll of 25,000 to 50,000 Iraqi Troops," *New York Times,* 1 March 1991, A1; Freedman and Karsh, "How Kuwait Was Won," 37n; and Brown and Shukman, *All Means Necessary,* 191.

77. "Report: Allies Faced Only 183,000 Iraqis," *Washington Post,* 24 April 1992, A25.

78. "Census Bureau to Dismiss Analyst Who Estimated Iraqi Casualties," *New York Times,* 7 March 1992, 9; "Census Bureau Retracts Firing of Researcher," *Washington Post,* 12 April 1992, A5.

79. Louise Cainkar, "Desert Sin: A Post-War Journey Through Iraq," in *Beyond the Storm,* ed. Bennis and Moushabeck.

80. "Allies Accused of Breaking Rules of War," *Manchester Guardian Weekly,* 24 November 1991, 10. See also Joost R. Hilterman, "Bomb Now, Die Later," *Mother Jones,* July/August 1991; and Jessica Mathews, "A New Meaning for the Term 'Germ Warfare'," *Manchester Guardian Weekly,* 28 April 1991, 19. For a discussion of the diplomatic debates surrounding Protocol 1, during which the United States refused to acknowledge the civilian nature of electricity facilities, see Arkin, Durrant, and Cherni, *On Impact,* 125.

81. Arkin, Durrant, and Cherni, *On Impact,* 44.

82. Arkin, Durrant, and Cherni, *On Impact,* 107–111, 131–132.

83. Quoted in Brown and Shukman, *All Means Necessary,* 154–155.

84. Brown and Shukman, *All Means Necessary,* 193.

85. Arkin, Durrant, and Cherni, *On Impact,* 45.

86. Barbara Ehrenreich, "The Panama Paradigm," in *Beyond the Storm,* ed. Bennis and Moushabeck, 89. In Panama, the estimates of civilian deaths ranged from 202 (the official U.S. figure) to 4,000 as claimed by some Panamanians and U.S. human rights groups.

87. "U.S. Bombs Missed 70% of Time," *Washington Post,* 16 March 1991, A1. The notion of a "miss" needs some qualification, however, to distinguish what some have called the colloquial understanding from the military understanding. While it might be assumed that each miss results in what the military calls "collateral damage," the definitions of accuracy employed by the armed forces have been getting more stringent, so that what was once a hit because it landed in a 200-meter radius on the military target, is now a miss because it lands outside a 20-meter radius on the military target. See Arkin, Durrant, and Cherni, *On Impact,* 82.

88. Arkin, Durrant, and Cherni, *On Impact,* 78; Brown and Shukman, *All Means Necessary,* x.

89. Arkin, Durrant, and Cherni, *On Impact,* 80. After the war, the chief of the air force revealed that he had seen unreleased video footage of smart weapons missing their target. Arkin, Durrant, and Cherni, *On Impact,* 14. For eyewitness accounts of such occurrences in civilian areas in Baghdad, see "Myth of Pinpoint Bombing," *The Independent,* 14 February 1991, 1; "No Hiding Place for a Nation Living Under Bombardment," *The Independent,* 4 February 1991, 3; "Cruise Missiles Killing Civilians in Iraqi Capital," *The Independent,* 2 February 1991, 1. These reports, made by Patrick Cockburn, were not subject to censorship.

90. "Allies Sought Wide Damage in Air War," *Manchester Guardian Weekly,* 30 June 1991, 18.

91. Arkin, Durrant, and Cherni, *On Impact,* 20, 75.

92. United Nations, *Report to the Secretary General on Humanitarian Needs in Kuwait and Iraq,* 5.

93. Moreover, even if Iraq were allowed to trade freely (something that UN

resolutions and sanctions currently prohibit), paying for these repairs could increase Iraqi indebtedness by the end of the 1990s to between $100 billion and $170 billion. "Hussein's Ouster is U.S. Goal, But at What Cost to the Iraqis?" *New York Times,* 28 April 1991, E1; and "U.S. Officials Believe Iraq Will Take Years to Rebuild," *New York Times,* 3 June 1991, A1.

94. "US Generals Divided Over Baghdad Raid," *The Independent,* 15 February 1991, 1; and Arkin, Durrant, and Cherni, *On Impact,* 92. For other accounts of the nonmilitary nature of the shelter, see Brown and Shukman, *All Means Necessary,* 53–55; and Simpson, *From the House of War,* 328–331. Robert Fisk's report of this incident in *The Independent* demonstrated how journalists operating outside the military pool system were able to obtain—even from official background sources—stories more significant than those written by their counterparts who accepted the military's censorship. For Fisk's reflections on this situation, see "Free to Report What We Are Told."

95. Arkin, Durrant, and Cherni, *On Impact,* 20, 94–98, 125–127.

96. "Allies Are Said to Choose Napalm For Strikes on Iraqi Fortifications," *New York Times,* 23 February 1991, 8. There have been some reports (though later questioned by U.S. officials) that Iraqi forces used chemical weapons, including napalm, during the civil war that followed the ceasefire. Arkin, Durrant, and Cherni, *On Impact,* 142–143.

97. Arkin, Durrant, and Cherni, *On Impact,* 20, 121–125, 138–139.

98. Friedrich, ed., *Desert Storm,* 3.

5

Sustaining Sovereignty
and the Politics of Principle

It looked enough like a country.

In his account of the discourse surrounding the conflict with Japan during World War II, historian John Dower remarked: "The propagandistic deception lies, not in the false claims of enemy atrocities, but in the pious depiction of such behavior as peculiar to the other side."[1] In these terms, the war with Iraq was rife with propagandistic deception on the part of the United States. At every opportunity—whether it concerned the status of the international boundary between Iraq and Kuwait, the conduct of the war, the grievances that lay behind it, the diplomatic opportunities that might have existed, or the human suffering and abuses of rights to which the conflict gave rise—the United States painted the issue in black and white terms when it was in actuality washed in shades of gray.

This conclusion holds for two of the major rationales for the war not discussed above: the view that Iraq posed a threat to control of the world's oil supply and the belief that it had nuclear ambitions. Each of these issues can be rendered in a manner that demonstrates how—contrary to the administration's rhetoric—the United States cannot be divorced from the problem in a fashion that locates the responsibility for evil with the Other. In the case of oil, the threat of an unfriendly hegemon in the Gulf is an issue for the United States principally because it has abandoned a national energy policy and doubled its reliance on imported oil in the last decade.[2] In the case of nuclear weapons proliferation, one can argue that because the superpowers did not until recently keep their part of the bargain in the Nuclear Non-Proliferation Treaty (to undertake sustained disarmament in exchange for control of proliferation), virtue in this matter cannot be located exclusively with one agent over another. Furthermore, the response of the United States to other instances of nuclear proliferation—in Pakistan, for example—has often been to ignore the matter when other strategic issues are deemed more important. Moreover, war with Iraq as an instrument of nonproliferation policy may have sent the wrong message. One Indian general has remarked that the conflict demonstrated that a country should not take on the United States unless it possesses nuclear weapons.[3]

In this context, faced with an abundance of ambiguity, the discourse of moral certitude—which engendered a belief in moral absolutism on the part of the United States and its allies—inscribed a series of boundaries between "us" and "them," "self" and "other," where none naturally existed. Indeed, the performative constitution of a complex array of boundaries (both ethical and territorial) designed to secure the identity and purpose of the United States and its allies was one of the major effects of the war. The discursive and political practices employed by the United States and its allies during the rite of passage to war—and the subsequent narrative enunciation of the war as well—worked to sustain state sovereignty in an environment where it was (and is) constantly challenged, transgressed, erased, and reinscribed.

There are many "lessons" to be drawn from this reading of the war with Iraq. For example, it suggests that just-war theory is woefully inadequate as a concept for anything other than the rationalization of war. Indeed, as Geyer and Green conclude, the Gulf War demonstrates that just-war theory is an ethic of war and not a complete ethic of war and peace.[4] Interestingly, Michael Walzer has affirmed this conclusion, perhaps unintentionally, in his assessment that while the experience of the Gulf War demonstrates the "conceptual inadequacy" of the maxims of last resort, discrimination, and proportionality, just-war theory "still does important work here, making it possible to defend some acts of war and to condemn others." Walzer's use of just-war theory as a rationalization of war is most evident in the way he effectively abandons the criterion of last resort, for he argues that if a war like that with Iraq was justified in the first instance at the time of the original invasion, it remains just whether or not there has been any attempt to avoid it in the interregnum.[5]

Other facets of the conflict equally render just-war theory inadequate. For example, because of developments in the technology of war, notions such as discrimination and proportionality have been stripped of their original intentions. While those who planned this war trumpeted their concern for accuracy with the intent of minimizing "collateral damage," it turned out, as was shown in Chapter 4, that the targeting discrimination of smart weapons during the war led to a *disproportionate* number of civilian casualties after the war—unless one considers the tens of thousands of deaths to have been in proportion to the success of "surgical" strikes. Likewise, the war has left in its wake many questions of a fundamental nature—among others, the future of diplomacy given the "success" of militarism, the role and performance of the media in crisis situations, and the state of our prospects for halting weapons proliferation. I want to argue, however, that few questions are more important to consider than the costs of conducting politics according to principle.

Posing the issue in these terms uncovers a startling paradox. The received view in realist theory and practice in international politics is that the conduct of foreign policy is impervious to questions of ethics and morality. (Consider, for example, how the literature is structured in terms of ethics *and* international relations.) As one writer has argued, "International politics, more than municipal or national politics, is resistant to the binding force of laws and norms, in part because of the weight of national sovereignty."[6] Echoing this position, George Kennan wrote in 1985, "The interests of the national society for which government has to concern itself are basically those of its military security, the integrity of its political life, and the well-being of its people. These needs have no moral quality."[7]

The impression that policy is driven by an amoral, objectivist criterion called "national interest" is encouraged by the way realism's positivist bias relegates normative concerns to a subsidiary status.[8] Yet, it is not difficult to discern in the literature that "the national interest" and its associated formulations cloak an ethical position mandated by the hierarchy of values allied with the notion of "reason of state."[9] Indeed, far from dispensing with questions of ethics and issues of morality altogether, conventional international relations literature makes it clear that realism has a particular ethical disposition associated with the integrity and security of the state. As Nardin notes, "As a moral argument, realism amounts to a claim that the reasons for overriding the constraints of ordinary morality in emergency situations are themselves moral."[10]

This is not to suggest that this literature is without its tensions, such as the longstanding debate between deontological and consequentialist conceptions of ethics, in which (for example) Hans Morgenthau strenuously resisted the former position and Niebuhr modified the latter in terms of practicality.[11] Nevertheless, for all the differences between those contending views, the dominant perspectives on ethics and international relations rest upon a couple of pivotal assumptions. The first is that states are largely self-contained entities, the ethical disposition of which is grounded internally rather than externally. As Charles Beitz has written, "Like persons in domestic society, states in international society are to be treated as autonomous sources of ends, morally immune from external interference, and morally free to arrange their internal affairs as their governments see fit."[12] The analogy is extended such that when the autonomous moral individual becomes the analog for the autonomous moral state, agents are separated from their actions, and states are moral only insofar as they are autonomous.[13] The second assumption is that an effective and proper morality requires careful delineation of universal codes, laws, and rules designed to encourage some form of behavior and proscribe others. As Stanley Hoffman has argued, "A complete morality must not only include isolated behavioral prescriptions, but also set forth a comprehensive and systematic set of behavioral prescriptions that assist in guiding all human action."[14] These two assumptions are closely allied, for the idea that ethics is dependent upon a clearly identifiable moral code only makes sense insofar as there is a recognizably autonomous agent from whom that code derives and in whose service it can be deployed. The Gulf War, however, stands as a challenge to these assumptions and to the conventional understanding of ethics and international relations they inform.

The war with Iraq revealed how orthodox international political practice is premised upon an ethical principle—the principle of sovereignty.[15] At every turn, the prosecution of the war was made possible by a widely held belief that the necessity for clear and secure boundaries is the metaphysical a priori of a world in which territorial integrity and political independence exist as absolute values. Even traditions of thought as seemingly disparate as just-war theory and balance-of-power formulations share an unwavering commitment to the politics of principle insofar as they invoke the sanctity of the border.[16] Given the resentment, revenge, and orgiastic enactment of violence evidenced in the war with Iraq, however, we have to ask whether we can afford a politics enabled by the principle of sovereignty. Moreover, we have to ask whether or not the realist's commitment to the principle of sovereignty is (ironically) an instance of idealism in our postmodern world, where the rigid defense of sovereign communities located in a radically interdependent economy of violence could exacerbate many of the perils from which we seek to be secure. In other words, we have to ask whether or not the problematization of the state as an autonomous moral agent is accurate in its ethnographic claims about contemporary global politics; and whether or not the understanding of ethics here, as a register of rules allied to that autonomy, defeats itself by encouraging violence through its attribution of responsibility. A number of features peculiar to the Gulf War highlight these concerns.

Of all territories upon which to stake a defense of the principle of sovereignty, Kuwait was one of the most precarious. Although commentators such as Michael Walzer made short shrift of the issue (declaring it looked enough like a country), Kuwait nonetheless existed along dimensions other than that of territoriality. While its huge oil reserves provided a measure of economic viability missing in many other states (small or large), it nonetheless remained a state dependent upon cliency relationships that compromised any sense of absolute sovereignty.[17] Moreover, although it can be said that political authorities in Kuwait had control over its economic resources, in another sense, Kuwait was no more than "a small albeit major subassembly in the transnational machinery of global energy markets."[18] Indeed, as a state that earned billions of dollars each year in "electronically accumulated wealth" from "off-shore" investments, Kuwait—perhaps more so than most states—could be located along a temporal (or chronopolitical) dimension as readily as in a spatial (or geopolitical) register.[19] Accordingly, while Iraq—thinking traditionally in terms of the importance of sovereignty—seized territory in order to capture or obtain leverage over wealth, it found Kuwait to be somewhere other than it appeared. As Timothy Luke argues, "Even as Kuwait as 'the place in space' was being annexed, or deterritorialized, Kuwait as 'a stream in flow' simply changed its passwords, recoded its access protocols to open at other nodes, and respecified its service-delivery points."[20]

Yet, no matter how unique Kuwait was in the degree of its capacity to refigure the bases of its sovereignty, its ability to do so was something many if not all states share. For example, Iraq managed to equip and finance its militarization plans by using the non-national and deterritorialized nature of capital and industry to its advantage. As Chapter 3 detailed, Iraq assembled a complex and extensive network of relationships for the procurement of military technology, none of which derived their legitimacy from a territorial identification, and none of which can be understood in conventional terms as wholly private or public. Moreover, what Iraq did was not an exception in this era of globalized capitalism; its practices embodied what is now the norm, albeit a norm poorly understood by our traditional modes of interpretation.

In addition to the contingent nature of Kuwait and the character of Iraqi militarization, the prosecution of the Gulf War manifested another instance of the tension between the impulses of sovereignty and exchange.[21] While the United States sought to exercise its national military power, it relied upon international economic power to make that exercise possible. Unable and/or unwilling to foot the bill for a strategy it devised, the United States insured funding for the military conflict through a global coalition of economic resources assembled under the umbrella of the Gulf War Financial Coordination Committee. Much of the secretary of state's diplomatic activity in the period approaching January 1991 involved soliciting monetary grants from countries around the world—an exercise derisively labelled "tin-cup diplomacy"; the United States was thus able to secure more than enough contributions (totalling $54.6 billion) to pay for the war.[22] Of the total amount pledged by allies (more than 90 percent of which was paid in the first half of 1991 alone), $49 billion was in cash, with the remainder consisting of in-kind contributions of material. The cash amount fully covered the cost of the war, which totalled $31.6 billion to the time of the ceasefire at the end of February 1991. Indeed, at that point, the United States might be considered to have made a "profit" of over $17 billion on the war. This "profit" was then spent on postcombat redeployment and phasedown operations, which cost $12.2 billion. The remainder seems to have been spent on an additional amount of unspecified costs (but thought to include equipment repair and replacement) that the Office of Management and Budget calculated somewhat mysteriously after the war. The total cost to U.S. taxpayers of Operation Desert Shield-cum-Storm and the Kurdish relief operation was no more than $2.7 billion beyond the money already appropriated for the defense budget, a fraction of the $15 billion Congress authorized for the mission in 1991. In other words, countries other than the United States paid some 95 percent of the costs associated with the conflict after August 1990, thereby giving a new meaning to the term "burden sharing," and putting the bases of economic and military sovereignty into tension.

These reflections on sovereignty indicate that in this postmodern world, where chronoeconomic processes exist in tension with geopolitical formations, such that the latter are always contingent, we need to disaggregate the state's function as *the primary locus of identity* from its putative role as *the exhaustive site of control.* This is not to suggest that tensions between chronoeconomic processes and geopolitical formations are unique to the recent epoch we describe as postmodern. On the contrary—as Thompson and Krasner have argued—because orthodox interpretive practices "ignored the difficulties that states have always encountered" in maintaining their sovereignty, the supposed novelty of this period is dependent upon the notion that there was "some golden age in the past . . . [in which states had] been able to effortlessly control transborder movements."[23] In the contemporary era, however, the extent and nature of the vast network of relations within which states are sequestered as subjects disturb the efficaciousness of any one-dimensional representation of agency, power, responsibility, or sovereignty. Accordingly, security in the postmodern world cannot only (or even primarily) be about territorial boundaries and the ethical borders that instantiate them.

This is not to suggest that territoriality is without importance for politics. The issue at hand is not one of temporal flows replacing spatial forces, but the way in which chronoeconomic processes denaturalize geopolitical representations, such that we can think of the state (and other loci of identity) in terms of the effects of ongoing practices of deterritorialization and reterritorialization.[24] Again, this theme was materialized in the conduct of the Gulf conflict. The deployment of high-tech weaponry and the accelerated destruction it enabled meant that for Iraq security was disengaged from territory. In facing a war that "from lack of space, spread out into Time," survival for Iraq involved duration rather than geography. Indeed, because the all-terrain (or, as Virilio notes, the sans-terrain) nature of assault "extends war over an earth that disappears, crushed under the infinity of possible trajectories,"[25] Iraq's reliance on conventional strategic dispositions merely hastened its defeat. As Jonathan Schell observed during the conflict, "The Iraqis' land (and the land of Kuwait, which they unjustly seized) had become their cage."[26]

Although deterritorialized during the war, Iraq was reterritorialized in its aftermath, albeit in a manner that demonstrated the way in which sovereignty operates in terms of hierarchies of authority as much as ledgers of space. Theorists indebted to a one-dimensional (spatial) understanding of sovereignty regard the transformation of a state's internal politics as an unwarranted "usurpation of sovereignty" to be condemned in the same manner as aggression.[27] Yet the same countries that had gone to war against Iraq for its violation of Kuwait's sovereignty openly and willingly breached Iraq's autonomy as part of the postwar settlement. With a series of Security Council resolutions designed to discipline Iraq's economic and security practices well into the future—through the maintenance of the same sanctions only months earlier declared to be ineffective, and via the establishment of an arrangement of suzerainty to protect the Kurds in northern Iraq and the Shiites in the south—the victors of the Gulf conflict transgressed the sovereignty of space so as to instantiate the sovereignty of control.

Representing these practices and processes is fraught with complications. Most obviously, we are hampered in our efforts to disentangle the complex relationships of flows and spaces, authority and territory, chronopolitics and geopolitics, by the fact that modern policy discourses—particularly international relations—enunciate a "state-centric grammar" indebted to the sovereignty problematic.[28] Not only is sovereignty an artifice designed to explain juridical or territorial power; it is also an interpretive disposition implicated in those same explanations. Sovereignty, as Derrida noted, "is presence, and the delight in presence."[29] This feature is not exclusive to the discipline of international relations; on the contrary, the sovereignty problematic is an almost ubiquitous cultural practice in societies such as ours.[30] In this general sense, it is manifested in what Stephen White has termed the "metanarrative of subjectivity": "the awareness of how strongly Western thought is oriented to the consciousness of a subject (singular or collective) who is faced with the task of surveying, subduing, and negotiating *his* way through a world of objects, other subjects, and his own body."[31]

Whether we characterize the issue in White's terms or in terms of

Derrida's metaphysics of presence and logocentrism, this dimension of sovereignty points to the way in which we require some secure subject, ground, or foundation upon which to anchor our knowledge, even if that secure subject is at odds with what it is we are trying to understand. Moreover, this dimension of sovereignty directs us toward a rethinking of agency in more fluid terms. As Judith Butler has argued:

> Agency belongs to a way of thinking about persons as instrumental actors who confront an external political field. But if we agree that politics and power exist already at the level at which the subject and its agency are articulated and made possible, then agency can be *presumed* only at the cost of refusing to inquire into its construction. . . . In a sense, the epistemological model that offers us a pregiven subject or agent is one that refuses to acknowledge that *agency is always and only a political prerogative.*[32]

In the context of international relations the sovereignty problematic points to the manner in which most if not all processes—whether related to questions of identity or of control—are conflated and rendered in terms of the state as agent and author, and if not the state, then some other purportedly secure agent such as the corporation. It is hard to escape this discourse: for example, I have often in this essay referred to "U.S. corporations" and "German companies" when examining the web of relationships brought into view by the Gulf War. Such designations, however, are questionable because they conflate the *company* with the *country,* and vice versa. In so doing, they resolve the ambiguous and contested nature of agency behind policy in a particular manner, such that "international relations" come to be articulated solely in geostrategic terms, thereby marginalizing the agency and importance of capital, corporations, private, and quasiprivate relations (among many others).

Moreover, the disjunction and tension between identity and control now facing the state is facing other agents as well—in particular, the corporation—such that any rendering of global economic relations in terms of the sovereignty problematic is equally flawed. Indeed, although both academic and popular economic literature represent the corporation as an autonomous agent, Robert Reich has argued that "this grammar perpetuates a subtle but pervasive deception," for there is no longer any distinction between the "inside" and the "outside" of a corporation.[33] What we think is an autonomous agent called a corporation, Reich argues, should instead be understood as a node in a complex global enterprise web. For example, although we think of Chrysler, Ford, and GM as names of corporations that produce cars, in fact, much if not most of the value of the cars bearing their names is produced "outside" their manufacturing sites. Because of the trend toward outsourcing and subcontracting in global enterprise webs, the Chrysler Corporation directly produces only 30 percent of the value of its cars; for Ford the figure is 50 percent; while GM buys half of its engineering and design services from eight hundred different companies. In other words, developments such as these mean "the space of organizations in the informational economy is increasingly a *space of flows*."[34] In consequence, a changing spatialization of corporate power has disturbed established political spatializations, but this transformation has been opaque to the dominant representations of space and power within the discipline of international relations.

What is required, then, is a mode of representation in which the complex nature of agency and responsibility is neither elided nor occluded by the sovereignty problematic; we need a "deterritorialization of theory" such that interpretation and understanding no longer depend upon a single site of meaning in which to ground truth;[35] and we need an account of ethics and responsibility that can inform contemporary international political practice but that is no longer dependent upon the unsustainable notion of autonomous agency for its authority. Although the development of a mode of representation that goes beyond the sovereignty problematic is beyond the scope of this essay,[36] I take up the question of ethics and agency in the next chapter.

NOTES

The epigraph that opens this chapter is quoted from Walzer, "On Just Wars," 42.

1. Dower, *War Without Mercy*, 12.
2. For an analysis, see Lovins and Lovins, *Making Fuel Efficiency Our Gulf Strategy*.
3. Remark by George Rathjens, Five College Program in Peace and World Security Studies Winter Faculty Workshop, Amherst College, 15 January 1992.
4. Geyer and Green, *Lines in the Sand*, 24.
5. Walzer, *Just and Unjust Wars*, 2d ed., xiii, xv, xxi.
6. Thompson, *Morality and Foreign Policy*, 8.
7. Quoted in McElroy, *Morality and American Foreign Policy*, 27.
8. Frost, *Towards a Normative Theory of International Relations*.
9. Smith, *Realist Thought from Weber to Kissinger*, Chapter 9; and Terry Nardin, "Ethical Traditions in International Affairs," in *Traditions of International Ethics*, ed. Nardin and Mapel.
10. Nardin, "Ethical Traditions in International Affairs," 15.
11. McElroy, *Morality and American Foreign Policy*, 25. On Niebuhr's practical morality, see Thompson, *Morality and Foreign Policy*, 181ff.
12. Quoted in Warner, *An Ethic of Responsibility in International Relations*, 37.
13. Warner, *An Ethic of Responsibility in International Relations*, 45.
14. Quoted in McElroy, *Morality and American Foreign Policy*, 38. See also Pogge, "Liberalism and Global Justice."

15. By "orthodox" I mean those perspectives and practices indebted to an epistemic realism. The term includes, for example, the tenets of liberalism that stem from John Locke and underpin both just-war theory and Hedley Bull's conception of anarchical society. Indeed, much of the logic behind the Gulf crisis—particularly the demonizing of those who transgress the principles of reason important to a community—resonate with Locke's rendition of the state of nature. As Locke wrote: "a criminal, who, having renounced reason, the common rule and measure God hath given mankind, hath . . . declared war against all mankind . . . may be destroyed as a lion or a tiger, one of those wild savage beasts with whom men can have no society nor security." Locke, *Two Treatises of Government,* Chapter 2, 27.

16. See the discussion of Walzer's just-war theorizing above. For balance-of-power theorists, the act of crossing a border increases a nation's power and vitiates any relations one may have had with the aggressor. Accordingly, they argue there was nothing inconsistent in U.S. policy tilting to and fro between Iran and Iraq throughout the 1980s. Therefore—even though such thinkers overtly remove moral considerations from their calculus—they adopt a position that, because of its faith in sovereignty, is highly principled. For an example of this, see Friedman, *Desert Victory,* 28–29.

17. Tetreault, "Autonomy, Necessity, and the Small State."

18. Luke, "The Discipline of Security Studies and the Codes of Containment," 324.

19. Luke, "The Discipline of Security Studies and the Codes of Containment," 317–325. Quotes are at 324–325. The idea of chronopolitics comes from the work of Paul Virilio. For its importance to international relations, see Der Derian, "The (S)pace of International Relations."

20. Luke, "The Discipline of Security Studies and the Codes of Containment," 325.

21. Shapiro, "Sovereignty and Exchange." The idea of sovereignty/exchange is developed by Shapiro to consider the tensions of geopolitics/chronoeconomics.

22. Defense Budget Project, *Desert Shield/Storm Costs and FY 1991 Funding Requirements.* While Japan was subjected to intense public criticism about its perceived failure to provide substantial support, Schwarzkopf reveals in his book that were it not for the quiet but timely transfer of tens of millions of dollars from the Japanese embassy in Riyadh to the U.S. Central Command's accounts, Operation Desert Shield would have been without money in August 1990. Schwarzkopf, *It Doesn't Take a Hero,* 365.

23. Janice E. Thompson and Stephen D. Krasner, "Global Transactions and the Consolidation of Sovereignty," in *Global Changes and Theoretical Challenges,* ed. Czempiel and Rosenau, 197.

24. This theme comes from Deleuze and Guattri, *A Thousand Plateaus.* It is discussed in Shapiro, "Sovereignty and Exchange," 469–470. As Paul Virilio observes, "The problem is no longer one of a historiality in (chronological) time or (geographic) space, but in what space-time?" Virilio, *Speed and Politics,* 117.

25. Virilio, *Speed and Politics,* 56.

26. Quoted in Arkin, Durrant, and Cherni, *On Impact,* 147.

27. Walzer, *Just and Unjust Wars,* 2d ed., xvii.

28. Shapiro, *Reading the Postmodern Polity,* especially Chapter 7.

29. Derrida, *Of Grammatology,* 296.

30. See Ashley, "Living on Border Lines: Man, Poststructuralism, and War," in *International/Intertextual Relations,* ed. Der Derian and Shapiro.

31. White, *Political Theory and Postmodernism,* 6.

32. Judith Butler, "Contingent Foundations: Feminism and the Question of Postmodernism," in *Feminists Theorize the Political,* ed. Butler and Scott, 13.

33. Reich, *The Work of Nations,* 102.

34. Castells, *The Informational City,* 169.

35. Der Derian, "Videographic War II," 11.

36. I have developed this theme further in relation to representations of world politics in Campbell, "Prosaics of Order."

6

Ethical Engagement and the Practice of Foreign Policy

RETHINKING ETHICS

For many the idea of deterritorializing theory, of moving away from supposedly secure grounds and reportedly rock-like foundations, amounts to an abandonment of principle and an advocacy of anarchy. Even among those who acknowledge that an indebtedness to the politics of principle brought us the slaughter of the Gulf War, some feel uneasy about discarding what they understand to be a necessary moral compass. Aside from the arguable premise of such a view—that we have had or are in possession of uncontested foundations as the basis for our way of life—the point I wish to make is this: abandoning principle does not mean jettisoning ethics, and advocating anarchy does not mean acquiescing to disorder and injustice. Indeed, it is the conviction of this essay that it is possible to articulate an ethico-political disposition that is both consonant with the complexities of the postmodern world and capable of encouraging us to resist undemocratic practices.[1]

Moreover, given the restructuring of social and political theory in recent times, not only is it possible to recast ethics in these terms; the task is overdue.[2] Of course, the conception of ethics that emerges from this reconsideration is different from that normally associated with the word, at least in the metaphysical tradition of philosophy and the conventional international relations literature it informs. There, ethics is most often understood in terms of the rules of conduct or the moral code that undergirds, through various commands, the path to a good and just life. But in the wake of the Heideggerian critique, the ground for moral theory has been removed, because the *ethos* of moral philosophy cannot remain once the *logos* of metaphysics has gone.[3] A key to this reconsideration lies in the Greek etymology of "anarchy." *An-arche* means "being without first principle": in as much as political theory has gone beyond metaphysics to recognize the relational character

91

of subjectivity, it has revealed that "exchange deprived of principle" is the essence of praxis.[4] In the move beyond metaphysics, ethics has been transformed from something independent of subjectivity—that is, from a set of rules and regulations adopted by autonomous agents—to something insinuated within and integral to that subjectivity. Accordingly, ethics is not ancillary to the existence of a subject (whether that subject be a person, a state, or some other figuration of identity); ethics is indispensable to the very being of that subject, because a subject's being is only possible once its *right to be* in relation to the Other is claimed. This recasting of the issue refigures the moral economy in which responsibility is assigned.

It is in the work of Emmanuel Levinas that this interpretation finds its best expression, because for Levinas being is a radically interdependent condition, a condition made possible only because of my responsibility to the Other.[5] Levinas's philosophy points toward a sense of responsibility distant from that associated with Augustinian thinking and thus unlike what is usually articulated in foreign policy discourse.[6] It is a more fundamental sense of responsibility than that to which we are accustomed. It is "a responsibility without limits, and so necessarily excessive, incalculable, before memory . . . responsibility before the very concept of responsibility."[7] It is a responsibility that is preoriginal, anarchic, and devolved from an "infrastructural alterity";[8] thus it refigures our understanding of both subjectivity and ethics. It refigures subjectivity because the very origin of the subject is to be found in its subjection to the Other, a subjection that precedes consciousness, identity, and freedom.[9] In other words, subjects are constituted by their relationship with the Other. Their being is called into question by the prior existence of the Other. Moreover—and this is what refigures ethics—this relationship with the Other means that one's being has to be affirmed in terms of *a right to be* in relation to the Other.

Having decentered subjectivity by making it an effect of the relationship with the Other, Levinas's thought recasts ethics in terms of a primary responsibility that stakes our being upon the assertion of our right to be. As Levinas declares, "We name this calling into question of my spontaneity by the presence of the Other ethics."[10] In turn, the recasting of ethics reinforces the decentering of subjectivity.

For Levinas, the distinction between the ethical and the moral is one that is important to maintain, even though the two are intimately intertwined. While morality can be understood as the rules relating to social behavior (rules often invoked by those seeking to answer "why"), these "rules"—which are always more contingent than they appear—are never separated from our ethical responsibility toward the Other. In this sense, ethics does not decree rules for society. But for Levinas, while it is morality that governs society, it is ethics—as "the extreme sensitivity of one subjectivity to another," the heteronomous responsibility of our subjectivity—that governs morality.[11] The consequence of this is the recognition *that "we" are always already ethically situated; making judgments about conduct, therefore, depends less on what sort of rules are invoked as regulations, and more on how the interdependencies of our relations with others are appreciated.* To repeat one of Levinas's key points: "Ethics redefines subjectivity as this heteronomous responsibility, in contrast to autonomous freedom."[12]

RETHINKING ETHICS, INTERNATIONAL RELATIONS, AND THE GULF WAR

These reflections might appear at first glance to be distant from the concerns of international relations, U.S. foreign policy, and an examination of the Gulf War. Yet, to fit James Der Derian's thoughts into this frame, this is "not yet another utopian scheme to take us out of the 'real' world, but a practical strategy to live with less anxiety, insecurity, and fear . . . [so that] radical otherness in international relations is assumed and asserted in dialogue, not subsumed and repressed in violence."[13] As emerged tellingly in Chapters 3, 4, and 5, which called attention to episodes that disturb the dominant narrative of the war with Iraq, it was reliance on the politics of principle—empowered by the discourse of moral certitude—that worked to absolve the United States of responsibility for a crisis in which it was actively implicated. Whether we focus upon the geopolitical relationships that tied Iran, Iraq, Kuwait, and the United States together throughout the 1980s; whether we focus on the geoeconomic practices of the United States and its allies with regard to Iraq's industrial and military programs; or whether we focus on the chronoeconomic processes that existed in tension with the others; we have to conclude that the United States was always already ethically situated in relation to the issues and protagonists in the crisis. To be judged as having acted in an ethical way, it would have been more fitting for the United States to acknowledge this heteronomous responsibility than to assert its autonomous freedom.

Such an acknowledgment would not have hindered the Bush administration and its allies from taking a tough stance against Iraq's invasion of Kuwait. On the contrary, it would have equipped the United States and others with increased authority to resist the Iraqi action and work toward a resolution. Aside from the possibility—albeit conceivable only as a counterfactual proposition—that this disposition might have prevented the crisis in the first place by differently figuring U.S. policies throughout the region in the 1980s, this acknowledgment would most certainly have favored a diplomatic resolution of the crisis in the five months after the invasion. Given the economic context of debt, oil revenues, and international credit in which the Iraqi invasion was situated—and in which the United States and its allies were directly implicated—any acknowledgment of the complex interdependencies between the various agents would have reduced the pressures of sovereign identity that called for a definitive and violent resolution to the conflict.

This rendering of ethics does not demand that a state's foreign policy be unambiguous and thoroughly consistent. All it requires is that an appreciation for ambiguity and a sensitivity to contingency be built into foreign policy, such that the adversarial or the unexpected does not become an occasion for moral absolutism and violent retribution akin to the dark days of the Cold War. Indeed, it is one of the great ironies of the Gulf War that a crisis that was understood as the first of the post–Cold War era had its economic dimension buried in the rush to a military solution. We are left to conclude that the characteristic features of Cold War foreign policy—a sense of endangerment ascribed to the activities of the Other, a fear of internal challenge and subversion, a tendency to criminalize or militarize responses, a willingness to tightly draw the lines of superiority/inferiority between "us" and "them," and the representation of danger in the external realm such that sovereignty can be sustained—were related more to the logic of U.S. (and Western) identity than to the specific threat of the Soviet Union (or other Others).[14]

Redefining ethics in terms of heteronomous responsibility rather than autonomous freedom thus portends the possibility of finally laying the Cold War to rest. At the very least, for a world of deepening interconnections and accelerating interrelationships, this disposition in foreign policy might offer the prospect of an improved quality of life for many. What is the meaning of such a notion for the contemporary challenges facing U.S. foreign policy? What might this disposition mean for the conduct of international relations, were it adopted?

REFLECTIONS ON U.S. FOREIGN POLICY

Following the demise of the Soviet Union, and the strategic proclamation that uncertainty and unpredictability are the new enemies, U.S. foreign policy discourse is casting around for a new set of principles to guide action and aid judgment about the place of the United States in the world. Yet, for all the novelty of the situation, the debate associated with these developments is structured along traditional lines, as a battle between the advocates of "isolationism" and the proponents of "intervention."[15]

Strikingly, moreover, despite its appearance as a debate, the range of possibilities considered in this discourse is extremely narrow and somewhat predictable. In the absence of few actual champions of isolationism, the argument countering intervention is largely a mythical construction of an impossible position on the part of those who intend to disparage it. (The "idealists" of international relations theory were defined in a similar way by the "realists" seeking to counter them.) Likewise, while there is some disagreement over when national interests are at stake for the United States, there is little contention among those putatively at odds with one another that the United States must retain an internationalist policy.[16] While some justify this stance through an appeal to "American purpose" in the world, most argue that it is an inescapable reality in a time of increasing interdependence.[17]

To be sure, the practical exigencies of world politics in our time mean that interdependence is an unavoidable condition and autarky nothing more than an illusion, as, for example, Chapters 3 and 4 demonstrated with respect to the Gulf War. For a nation such as the United States, involvement in the world is not a matter of choice; the issue is what disposition toward the world it wants to adopt. This question is eclipsed in many of the current attempts to define a new role for the United States in the post–Cold War era. Indeed, in many analyses, recognition of the increasingly pervasive nature of interdependence opens the way to a position advocating increased (and often forcible) intervention, an argument that first came to prominence in the 1970s when balance-of-power thinking was under challenge from advocates of "world order" politics.[18] But is "involvement" necessarily synonymous with or the precursor to "intervention"? The discussion of ethics and subjectivity in this chapter suggests a very different conclusion, one that calls for humility rather than hubris in the face of interdependence. Specifically, by broadening our understanding of interdependence, I want to draw an important distinction between an agent's being-in-the-world and the modality of that being.

In international relations literature, interdependence is taken to be the result of empirical transactions between previously autonomous and sovereign states.[19] Notwithstanding the fact that those transactions are of importance, there is a prior and more fundamental sense of interdependence that is significant here: the sense in which the origin of an agent or subject—whether that agent or subject be an individual or a state—is to be found in the relationship between self and Other, and not in the uncovering of some autonomous sovereign ground of being removed from that relationship. This understanding has been the central theme of this essay, whether articulated in philosophical terms or demonstrated empirically through the complexity of the issues surrounding the Gulf War. Its importance for the debate about the U.S. role in the world cannot, I think, be underestimated. If we proceed from the basis of recognizing that the very being of a state like the United States derives from its relationship with the Other, that state is thus always already engaged with the Other and can feign neither ignorance about nor lack of interest in the Other's fate. In this sense, while "radical interdependence"—as I have termed it—is, philosophically speaking, the fundamental situation of a subject's being-in-the-world, the modality associated with that being is something to be politically contested and negotiated. In the place of intervention as that modality, I want to argue that *engagement* with the world is the foundation of an ethical disposition and the condition of possibility for a state's subjectivity.

Central to thinking in these terms is a different sense of responsibility. While international relations discourse is replete with the concept, it is usually discussed within the confines of the moral economy of culpability: who is responsible for this evil and thus subject to punishment, and who is responsible for undertaking that punitive action. In the terms outlined here, however, because responsibility to the Other is at the heart of one's subjectivity, regardless of the particular form that subjectivity takes, responsibility can neither be intentionally ascribed nor purposefully avoided. Indeed, because our sense of self is derived from our relationship with the Other and thus from our responsibility to the Other, to devolve responsibility to another or seek to evade it altogether is in actuality to deny an integral element of our-selves. Accordingly, in circumstances like those confronted in the Balkans and Somalia (among many others), to declare that inaction is appropriate because there are either no national interests at stake or no effective policy options available is to deny that each presents a challenge to the affirmation of life.[20] It is the idea of affirming life that is the important criterion—and perhaps, albeit ironically, the overriding principle—here; for in a situation of *an-arche,* of radical interdependence, one does not seek final justifications, or commands, or morals, or rationalizations, or answers to the "why" outside of life, beyond the nexus of being and acting.[21] One affirms the present, the life that one has, even in the most difficult of situations: as in the case of the cellist who memorialized twenty-two civilians killed in a mortar attack during the siege of Sarajevo by holding twenty-two solo performances of Albinoni's Adagio at the site of their deaths,[22] or the Orthodox Jew who, having prevented the lynching of a Palestinian after he had stabbed an Israeli boy in Jerusalem, lamented, "I protected someone because he was a human being, and found that I had to explain myself."[23]

This understanding is not a call for returning to an unproblematic humanism as a new ground upon which to anchor social and political life. Indeed, the affirmation of life as a predicate of being is to be distinguished from the argument—whether made implicitly or explicitly—that invokes "humanity" as a ground to fill the vacancy created when the notion of interdependence challenges state sovereignty. Though the values associated with the call to humanism are compatible with the affirmation of life, the call is nonetheless limited insofar as it attempts to replace one sovereign identity with another. This call has two attendant problems. First, those making such a call often seek to manufacture a new complex of principles, rules, and regulations designed to enforce their particular ethical position.[24] Second, and more importantly, the focus of concern here is the resentment and violence that flow from the principles required to secure an identity as sovereign. Simply changing the agent in whose name they operate does not disturb the more fundamental problem.[25]

To be engaged with the world, whether as an individual or a state, is thus a matter of acting in a way that seeks to affirm life. The specific nature of the plans, policies, or proclamations that can work toward this end require debate and negotiation attuned to the context they seek to address; they cannot be specified in the abstract. One important point can be made, however. Because of the pervasive influence of instrumental rationality upon international political discourse, action tends to be endorsed and embarked upon only when it can be said to clearly lead toward a solution. To be sure, the nature of the action and its chances for success are obviously important considerations. In the first instance, however, it is the fact of action in response to the recognition of one's engagement—though the action be no more than a strong declaration of one's position—that is the most important step. Again, this can be illustrated with respect to the crises in the Balkans. While both the European Community and the United States have undertaken limited policies to cope with the carnage (the Geneva negotiations, and the Clinton administration's appointment of an envoy to them), it is widely recognized that they have acted belatedly and sometimes half-heartedly to confront the barbarity of the conflict. Perhaps because they read the situation in terms of an implosion of sovereignty rather than a transgression of sovereignty—in contradistinction to the reasoning that spurred them to act in Kuwait—the articulation of responsibility has been heavily muted by publicly expressed doubts about what can be done; it is likely that these doubts have furthered the violence. Of course, we should think very seriously before embarking on such policies as the Bosnians' frequently requested commitment of military forces to combat in the area, but to use reasonable reservations about the most extreme option as grounds for doing little that is effective is nothing short of a denial of our unavoidable responsibility. Indeed, it can be argued that precisely because of our collective failure to acknowledge our prior responsibility to the Other, we have—as the case of dealing with Iraq forcefully demonstrated—backed ourselves into a corner such that military combat seems to be the only decisive (although undesirable) option. Had we in both cases recognized earlier our intrinsic interdependence with the problem we seek to handle, the range of choices might not have been so limited.

The major thrust of what I am trying to outline here is a different disposition to our being-in-the-world, such that the modalities through which we act upon that disposition do not perpetuate the violence they seek to avoid. Accordingly, I am calling for a different starting point, predicated on the relational character of subjectivity and on the sense of responsibility flowing from that. I am arguing that an appreciation for ambiguity and a sensitivity to contingency be built into foreign policy, in the hope that the alien, the foreign, and/or the unexpected does not become an occasion for moral absolutism and violent retribution. Of course, because states are paradoxical entities, and because foreign policy has acted so effectively as an ethical power of segregation—inscribing a particular geography of evil in order to fix a state's subjectivity—the argument here challenges many of the practices that have enabled us to live in supposedly secure and supposedly sovereign communities. Moreover, because it is not a policy manifesto with a catchy slogan that can be readily grasped by policymakers, many will complain that this argument does not supply the requisite principles to guide policy. This complaint, however, misses the central conclusion of the analysis of the Gulf War: that in our radically interdependent context, politics conducted in terms of a fixed principle such as sovereignty can exacerbate many of the perils from which we seek to be secure. Equally, it would be inaccurate to suggest that this argument leaves us incapable of formulating responses to some of the contemporary challenges facing the United States in the field of foreign policy. Although I do not offer a complete prescription here, I would argue that the disposition of ethical engagement in the world and the responsibility to the Other associated with it would mean:

1. Addressing the incidence of drug use at home without marginalizing consumers or militarizing the threat as foreign.
2. Thinking about how to handle the AIDS pandemic without scapegoating certain behaviors as immoral and without closing the frontiers to those who test HIV positive.
3. Conceiving of a means to address international trade problems without transmitting the fiscal pressures of the world economy to liminal groups within society, and without constituting the practices of one's competitors as responsible.
4. Reducing the tensions that give rise to political violence abroad while refraining from stigmatizing domestic political dissent as "terrorism,"
5. Implementing a national energy policy that uses a variety of ecologically sustainable technologies to reduce the dependence on imported oil and thus decreases the need to militarily secure its supply.
6. Controlling dual-use, high-technology, and nuclear exports to countries in situations of conflict or with poor human rights re-

cords.[26]

7. Providing adequate foreign aid even in times of economic recession, such that debts and dues for United Nations peacekeeping forces can be met.
8. Responding to the economic deprivation and political persecution of refugees by opening borders, disavowing repatriation, and deploying military forces on multilateral humanitarian missions under multinational command.

The list could go on and on, but there are two important features to this argument. The first is that in those cases where the focus is upon state action, it calls our attention to the genesis of the circumstances that function as the preconditions for such action. The second and perhaps most important feature of this argument is that it recognizes that foreign policy can be considered a practice of differentiation not restricted to (and in fact constitutive of) the domain of the state; it therefore seeks to encourage a commitment to politics through the articulation of a disposition to the world attuned to the political nature of agency and identity, rather than the identification of a fixed set of principles to be followed by supposedly autonomous and free subjects. While traditional perspectives on ethics and international relations have sought to specify in the abstract what good and right conduct consists of, such accounts inevitably offer, despite their desire to be concrete, no more than intangible formulations that are always subject to interpretation concerning their applicability.[27] The argument outlined here, by foregrounding the indispensability of interpretation in all these matters, does not shy away from the fact that these matters are always contested. Recognizing that "modernity . . . bequeaths to us a preference for *deriving* norms epistemologically over *deciding* them politically,"[28] this argument maintains that a hankering for the former is an avoidance of the latter, which neither is desirable nor can be sustained. Indeed, because engagement with the world is necessarily "global" in its scope, but the world is characterized by a multiplicity of agents none of whom can singlehandedly bear the burden of global responsibility, the way in which our ethical responsibility is to be acted upon has to be contested and negotiated. We have no choice but to make choices, even though all our choices are made from within and help to support a particular ethical disposition. However, were we to start by recognizing the way in which our responsibility to the Other is manifested in foreign policy, the task of affirming life might be better addressed.

NOTES

1. For further discussion, see David Campbell \ G. M. Dillon, "The Political

and the Ethical," in *The Political Subject of Violence,* ed. Campbell \ Dillon.

2. The literature on these developments in social and political theory is vast, but a useful starting point is Bernstein, *The Restructuring of Social and Political Theory;* and Bernstein, *The New Constellation.* For efforts to reconsider ethics in this context, see Caputo, *Radical Hermeneutics;* Cornell, *The Philosophy of the Limit;* Rajchman, *Truth and Eros;* Scott, *The Question of Ethics;* and Wyschogrod, *Saints and Postmodernism.*

3. Wyschogrod, *Saints and Postmodernism,* 191. For an introduction to Heidegger pertinent to these concerns, see Dreyfus, *Being-in-the-World.*

4. Schurmann, *Heidegger on Being and Acting,* 18.

5. Although the complexity and richness of Levinas's philosophy cannot be presented here, it is nonetheless important as a lever by which to open up a space for critical thought on ethics and international relations. The thoughts presented here are drawn from a number of sources, especially Emmanuel Levinas, "Ethics as First Philosophy," in *The Levinas Reader,* ed. Hand; and Levinas, *Totality and Infinity.* For an excellent discussion of Levinas on ethics, see Critchley, *The Ethics of Deconstruction.*

Reworkings of ethical thinking that have affinities to the themes of Levinas can be found in the recent books of Drucilla Cornell and Edith Wyschogrod. As Cornell argues:

> For my purposes, "morality" designates any attempt to spell out how one *determines* a "right way to behave," behavioral norms which, once determined, can be translated into a system of rules. The ethical relation, a term which I contrast with morality, focuses instead on the kind of person one must become in order to develop a nonviolent relationship with the Other. The concern of the ethical relation, in other words, is a way of being in the world that spans divergent value systems and allows us to criticize the repressive aspects of competing moral systems. (Cornell, *The Philosophy of the Limit,* 13.)

Wyschogrod writes that "ethics is the sphere of transactions between 'self' and 'Other' and is to be construed non-nomoligically . . . it cannot look to traditional philosophical discourse for a perspective on human conduct." Accordingly, she says, one must distinguish an ethic that appeals to alterity from one which leans on some conception of the good. Wyschogrod, *Saints and Postmodernism,* x, xv.

For a critique of Levinas's ethical thinking as a political theology designed to buttress Israel's sovereignty over Palestine, see Salemohamed, "Levinas."

6. On the Augustinian mode, see Connolly, *Identity/Difference,* Chapters 4 and 5.

7. Derrida, "Force of Law," 953, 955.

8. Critchley, "The Chiasmus," 96; and Fabio Ciaramelli, "Levinas's Ethical Discourse: Between Individuation and Universality," in *Re-Reading Levinas,* ed. Bernasconi and Critchley.

9. Ciaramelli, "Levinas's Ethical Discourse," 87.

10. Levinas, *Totality and Infinity,* 43.

11. Emmanuel Levinas and Richard Kearney, "Dialogue with Emmanuel Levinas," in *Face to Face with Levinas,* ed. Cohen, 29.

12. Levinas and Kearney, "Dialogue with Emmanuel Levinas," 27. Within international relations, the work of Daniel Warner goes some way toward this position, at least insofar as it invokes Martin Buber's I-Thou relationship to articulate a form of social morality in the ethics of international relations. See Warner, *An Ethic of Responsibility,* especially 20–21, 102–114. However, although

Buber's argument moves us toward Levinas, it leaves us some distance from him. This is clear in Levinas's critical commentary on Buber, where he notes that the I-Thou relationship is overly concerned with reciprocity, formality, and exclusiveness, such that a response (and, hence, responsibility) can only be obtained from a friendly partner in a reciprocal dialogue. It is thus a formal encounter, and not ethical in Levinas's sense. See Levinas, "Martin Buber and the Theory of Knowledge," in *The Levinas Reader,* ed. Hand.

13. Der Derian, "Videographic War II," 11.

14. See Campbell, *Writing Security.* These elements of "cold war-ism" were present during the Gulf crisis, and all except the issue of internal subversion are evident in the argument of this essay. There was, however, an important linkage of internal and external threats during this conflict. In addition to instances of discrimination against Arab-Americans, a broader sense of danger was also evoked. Charles Krauthammer argued in December 1990 (and was supported by commentators such as George Will) that the cultural contestation afoot in the United States—associated with the issues of multiculturalism, proliferating identities, changes in the educational curricula, "political correctness," postmodern discourses, etc.—is fragmenting the unity of society and "the American idea" to such an extent that the resultant "balkanization" poses "a threat that no outside agent in this post-Soviet world could match." While Krauthammer's argument declared that "America will survive . . . Saddam Hussein," it left the impression (in a manner reminiscent of Norman Podhoretz's arguments in the late 1970s) that this new catalog of internal subversives might weaken the country's vigilance toward the demons of the future. See Schulte-Sasse and Schulte-Sasse, "War, Otherness, and Illusionary Identifications," 78–83. Judith Butler pointed out to me one representation of this linkage: a November 1990 issue of *Newsweek* in which the cover story about political correctness ("The New Thought Police") was aligned with a photograph of Saddam Hussein.

15. Any number of articles could be cited as examples of this preoccupation, but for three randomly selected examples, see Francis Fukuyama, "The Beginning of Foreign Policy: America Confronts the Postwar World," *New Republic,* 17 and 24 August 1992; Special issue, "Superpower Without a Cause," *New Perspectives Quarterly* 9 (Summer 1992); and Gardner, "Practical Internationalism."

16. See "It's Harder Now to Figure Out Compelling National Interests," *New York Times,* 31 May 1992, E5.

17. For details of the way U.S. foreign policy has been invested with the notion of American purpose, see Campbell, *Writing Security,* especially Chapter 6.

18. This line of thought can be found as an implicit theme in Joseph Nye's recent reflections on the Gulf War: "Why the Gulf War Served the National Interest," *Atlantic Monthly,* 11 March 1992, especially 60. The struggle between balance-of-power and world order politics was a leitmotif of the Carter administration (in which Joseph Nye served). For details, see Campbell, *Security and Identity.* For a report that specified the reasons behind and strategies for intervention associated with interdependence, see Pauker, *Military Implications of a Possible World Order Crisis in the 1980s.*

19. One clear example that articulates this assumption is Holsti, "Change in the International System," in *Change in the International System,* ed. Holsti, Siverson, and George, 23. See also Mark W. Zacher, "The Decaying Pillars of the Westphalian Temple: Implications for International Order and Governance," in *Governance Without Government,* ed. Rosenau and Czempiel.

20. On the affirmation of life as a new predicate of being, see Campbell \

Dillon, "The Political and the Ethical."

21. It is for reasons similar to these that Wyschogrod focuses on the lives of saints in her effort to articulate a postmodern ethics. For Wyschogrod, a saint is defined not by a commitment to theistic standards, but by the living of a life committed to the reduction of pain or sorrow to others regardless of the cost to oneself. Accordingly, "In their disclosure of what is morally possible, saintly bodies 'fill' the discursive plane of ethics." Wyschogrod, *Saints and Postmodernism,* 34, 52. For a Nietzschean articulation of this theme that is behind these thoughts, see White, *Within Nietzsche's Labyrinth.*

22. "A People Under Artillery Fire Retain Bits of Their Humanity," *New York Times,* 8 June 1992, A1.

23. "Voices of Israel," *New York Times,* 8 June 1992, A10.

24. For a detailed argument that proposes a new value framework and associated principles, see Johansen, *The National Interest and the Human Interest.* While I agree with many of the dispositions articulated in this study, I would contest the assumptions associated with the sovereignty problematic throughout.

25. On this issue, see Roy, Walker, and Ashley, "Dialogue: Towards a Critical Social Theory of International Politics."

26. Amazingly, while exposé after exposé revealed how the United States was implicated in Iraqi militarization, the Bush administration eased the licensing requirements for military-related exports and encouraged the sale of such items to Iran and Syria. "Bush Eases Cold War Trade Curb," *New York Times,* 24 April 1992, D1; "U.S. to OK High-Tech Sales to Iran and Syria," *Los Angeles Times,* 13 February 1992, A1; and "Preventing the Next Saddam Hussein," *New York Times,* 15 March 1992, E16.

27. Stanley Hauerwas, "Whose Just War? Which Peace?" in *But Was It Just?* ed. Decosse, 86–87.

28. Brown, "Feminist Hesitations, Postmodern Exposures," 77.

Bibliography

BOOKS AND ARTICLES

Amnesty International. *Iraq: Evidence of Torture.* London: Amnesty International, 1981.
———. *Children: Innocent Victims of Political Repression.* New York: Amnesty International, 1989.
———. *Iraqi Kurds: At Risk of Forcible Repatriation from Turkey and Human Rights Violations in Iraq.* New York: Amnesty International, 1990.
———. *Iraq/Occupied Kuwait: Human Rights Violations Since August 2, 1990.* New York: Amnesty International, 1990.
Anderson, Ewan, and Khalil Rashidian. *Iraq and the Continuing Middle East Crisis.* New York: St Martin's Press, 1991.
Arkin, William W., Damian Durrant, and Marianne Cherni. *On Impact: Modern Warfare and the Environment, A Case Study of the Gulf War.* Washington, D.C.: Greenpeace, 1991.
Beitz, Charles R. *Political Theory and International Relations.* Princeton: Princeton University Press, 1979.
Benin, Joel. *Origins of the Gulf War.* Open Magazine Pamphlet Series No. 3. Westfield N.J.: Open Magazine, 1991.
Bennis, Phyllis, and Michel Moushabeck. *Beyond the Storm: A Gulf Crisis Reader.* New York: Olive Branch Press, 1991.
Bernasconi, Robert, and Simon Critchley, eds. *Re-Reading Levinas.* Bloomington: Indiana University Press, 1991.
Bernstein, Richard J. *The Restructuring of Social and Political Theory.* Philadelphia: University of Pennsylvania Press, 1976.
———. *The New Constellation: The Ethical-Political Horizons of Modernity/Postmodernity.* Cambridge: MIT Press, 1992.
Boot, William, "Operation Deep Think." *Columbia Journalism Review* (November/December 1990).
Brenner, Robert. "Why is the United States at War with Iraq?" *New Left Review* 185 (January/February 1991): 122–137.
Brittain, Victoria, ed. *The Gulf Between Us: The Gulf War and Beyond.* London: Virago Press, 1991.

Brown, Ben, and David Shukman. *All Means Necessary: Inside the Gulf War.* London: BBC Books, 1991.

Brown, Edward Hoagland. *The Saudi Arabia–Kuwait Neutral Zone.* Beirut: The Middle East Research and Publishing Center, 1963.

Brown, Peter G., and Henry Shue, eds. *Boundaries: National Autonomy and its Limits.* Totowa, NJ: Roman and Littlefield, 1981.

Brown, Wendy. "Feminist Hesitations, Postmodern Exposures." *differences: A Journal of Feminist Cultural Studies* 3 (1991): 63–84.

Brugger, Bill. "Was the Gulf War 'Just'?" *Australian Journal of International Affairs* 45 (November 1991): 161–168.

Bruner, Jerome. "The Narrative Construction of Reality." *Critical Inquiry* 18 (Autumn 1991): 1–21.

Bulloch, John, and Harvey Morris. *Saddam's War: The Origins of the Kuwait Conflict and the International Response.* London: Faber and Faber, 1991.

Butler, Judith, and Joan W. Scott. *Feminists Theorize the Political.* New York: Routledge, 1992.

Campbell, David. "Recent Changes in Social Theory: Questions for International Relations." In *New Directions in International Relations? Australian Perspectives,* edited by Richard A. Higgott. Canberra: Australian National University, 1988.

———. "Security and Identity: A Reading of the Carter Administration." Ph.D. diss., Australian National University, 1990.

———. *Writing Security: United States Foreign Policy and the Politics of Identity.* Minneapolis: University of Minnesota Press, 1992.

———. "Prosaics of Order: Transversal Politics in an An-Archical World," forthcoming.

Campbell, David, and Michael Dillon. "The Political and the Ethical." In *The Political Subject of Violence,* edited by David Campbell \ Michael Dillon. Manchester: Manchester University Press, 1993.

Caputo, John D. *Radical Hermeneutics: Repetition, Deconstruction, and the Hermeneutic Project.* Bloomington: Indiana University Press, 1989.

Carroll, David. *Paraesthetics: Foucault/Lyotard/Derrida.* New York and London: Methuen, 1987.

Castells, Manuel. *The Informational City: Information Technology, Economic Restructuring, and Urban-Regional Process.* Oxford: Basil Blackwell, 1989.

Chomsky, Noam. "After the Cold War: U.S. Foreign Policy in the Middle East." *Cultural Critique* 19 (Fall 1991): 15–31.

Chopra, Janet, and Thomas G. Weiss. "Sovereignty is No Longer Sacrosanct: Codifying Humanitarian Intervention." *Ethics and International Affairs* 6 (1992): 95–117.

Clark, Ramsey. *The Fire This Time: U.S. War Crimes in the Gulf.* New York: Thunders Mouth Press, 1992.

Clark, Ramsey, et al. *War Crimes: A Report on United States War Crimes Against Iraq.* Washington, D.C.: Maisonneuve Press, 1992.

Cloyd, J. Timothy, and Jean Bethke Elshtain, eds. *The Gulf War and Just War.* Study guide for the Retrospective on the Persian Gulf War conference, Vanderbilt University, 24–25 January 1992.

Cohen, Marshall D. "Moral Skepticism and International Relations." *Philosophy and Public Affairs* 13 (1984): 299–346.

Cohen, Richard A., ed. *Face to Face with Levinas.* Albany: State University of New York Press, 1986.

Connolly, William E. "Democracy and Territoriality." *Millennium: Journal of International Studies* 20 (Winter 1991): 463–484.

———. *Identity\Difference: Democratic Negotiations of Political Paradox.* Ithaca: Cornell University Press, 1991.

Cooley, John K. "Pre-War Gulf Diplomacy." *Survival* 33 (March/April 1991): 125–139.

Cornell, Drucilla. *The Philosophy of the Limit.* New York: Routledge, 1992.

Critchley, Simon. "The Chiasmus: Levinas, Derrida, and the Ethical Demand for Deconstruction." *Textual Practice* 3 (April 1989): 91–106.

———. *The Ethics of Deconstruction: Derrida and Levinas.* Oxford: Basil Blackwell, 1992.

Czempiel, Ernst-Otto, and James N. Rosenau, eds. *Global Changes and Theoretical Challenges: Approaches to World Politics for the 1990s.* Lexington: Lexington Books, 1989.

Decosse, David, ed. *But Was It Just?* New York: Random House, 1992.

Deleuze, Gilles, and Felix Guattri. *A Thousand Plateaus: Capitalism and Schizophrenia.* Translated by Brian Massumi. Minneapolis: University of Minnesota Press, 1987.

Der Derian, James. "The (S)pace of International Relations: Simulation, Surveillance, and Speed." *International Studies Quarterly* 34 (September 1990): 295–310.

———. "War Games May Prove Deadly." *Newsday,* 9 December 1990.

———. "Videographic War II." *Alphabet City* (Toronto), (Summer 1991): 4–12.

———. *Antidiplomacy: Spies, Terror, Speed, and War.* Cambridge, MA: Blackwells, 1992.

Der Derian, James, and Michael Shapiro, eds. *International/Intertextual Relations: Postmodern Readings in World Politics.* Lexington: Lexington Books, 1989.

Derrida, Jacques. *Of Grammatology.* Translated by Gayatri Chakravorty Spivak. Baltimore: Johns Hopkins University Press, 1976.

———. "But, beyond . . . (Open Letter to Anne Mclintock and Rob Nixon)." *Critical Inquiry* 13 (Autumn 1986): 155–170.

———. "Force of Law: The 'Mystical Foundation of Authority'," *Cardozo Law Review* 11 (July/August 1990): 919–1045.

Defense Budget Project. *Desert Shield/Storm Costs and FY 1991 Funding Requirements.* Washington, D.C.: Defense Budget Project, 1 July 1991.

Dillon, G. M. *The Falklands, Politics and War.* London: Macmillan, 1989.

———. *Defense, Discourse and Policy Making: Britain and the Falklands.* Institute on Global Conflict and Cooperation Working Paper No. 4. La Jolla: University of California, San Diego, 1988.

Doppelt, Gerald. "Walzer's Theory of Morality in International Relations." *Philosophy and Public Affairs* 8 (1978): 3–26.

———. "Statism without Foundations." *Philosophy and Public Affairs* 9 (Summer 1980): 399–403.

Dower, John. *War Without Mercy.* New York: Pantheon, 1986.

Dreyfus, Hubert L. *Being-in-the-World: A Commentary on Heidegger's "Being and Time," Division I.* Cambridge: MIT Press, 1991.

Drinnon, Richard. *Facing West: The Metaphysics of Indian Hating and Empire Building.* New York: Schocken Books, 1990.

Emerson, Steven A., and Cristina Del Sesto. *Terrorist.* New York: Villard Books, 1991.

Emery, Michael. *How Mr. Bush Got His War: Deceptions, Double Standards and*

Disinformation. Open Magazine Pamphlet Series No. 9. Westfield, NJ: Open Magazine, 1991.

Evangelista, Mathew. "Stalin's Postwar Army Reappraised." *International Security* 7 (1982/1983): 110–138.

Feldman, Allen. *Formations of Violence: The Narrative of the Body and Political Terror in Northern Ireland.* Chicago: University of Chicago Press, 1991.

Fialka, John J. *Hotel Warriors: Covering the Gulf War.* Washington, D.C.: Woodrow Wilson Center Press, 1992.

Foucault, Michel. *Power/Knowledge: Selected Interviews and Other Writings 1972–1977.* Edited by Colin Gordon. New York: Pantheon, 1980.

Freedman, Lawrence, and Efraim Karsh. "How Kuwait Was Won: Strategy in the Gulf War." *International Security* 16 (Fall 1991): 5–41.

Friedman, Norman. *Desert Victory: The War for Kuwait.* Annapolis: Naval Institute Press, 1991.

Friedrich, Otto, ed. *Desert Storm: The War in the Persian Gulf.* Boston: Time Warner, 1991.

Frost, Mervyn. *Towards a Normative Theory of International Relations.* Cambridge: Cambridge University Press, 1986.

Gardner, Richard N. "Practical Internationalism: The United States and Collective Security." *SAIS Review* 12 (Summer/Fall 1992): 35–49.

Garthoff, Raymond L. "Estimating Soviet Military Force Levels: Some Light From the Past." *International Security* 14 (1990): 93–116.

George, Jim. "International Relations and the Search for Thinking Space: Another View of the Third Debate." *International Studies Quarterly* 33 (1989): 269–279.

Geyer, Alan, and Barbara G. Green. *Lines in the Sand: Justice and the Gulf War.* Louisville: Westminster/John Knox Press, 1992.

Gottschalk, Marie. "Operation Desert Cloud: The Media and the Gulf War." *World Policy Journal* 9 (Summer 1992): 449–486.

Greenpeace. *Iraqi Deaths from the Gulf War as of December 1991.* Washington, D.C.: Greenpeace, 1991.

Halliday, Fred. "The Gulf War and its Aftermath: First Reflections." *International Affairs* 67 (April 1991): 223–234.

Helms, Christine Moss. *Iraq: Eastern Flank of the Arab World.* Washington, D.C.: The Brookings Institution, 1984.

Hermann, Richard K. "The Middle East and the New World Order: Rethinking U.S. Political Strategy After the Gulf War." *International Security* 16 (Fall 1991): 47–52.

Hiro, Dilip. *Desert Shield to Desert Storm: The Second Gulf War.* New York: Routledge, 1992.

Holmes, Robert L. *On War and Morality.* Princeton: Princeton University Press, 1989.

Holsti, Ole R., Randolph Siverson, and Alexander L. George, eds. *Change in the International System.* Boulder: Westview, 1980.

Jaber, Nadim. "Saudi Arabia Dampens Arab Peace Bids." *Middle East International,* 21 December 1990, 3–4.

Johansen, Robert C. *The National Interest and the Human Interest: An Analysis of U.S. Foreign Policy.* Princeton: Princeton University Press, 1980.

Johnson, James Turner, and George Weigel, eds. *Just War and the Gulf War.* Washington, D.C.: Ethics and Public Policy Center, 1991.

Jonas, Hans. *The Imperative of Responsibility: In Search of an Ethics for the*

Technological Age. Translated by Hans Jonas with the collaboration of David Herr. Chicago: University of Chicago Press, 1984.

Karsh, Efraim, and Inari Rautsi. "Why Saddam Hussein Invaded Kuwait." *Survival* 33 (January/February 1991): 18–30.

Kellner, Douglas. *The Persian Gulf TV War*. Boulder: Westview Press, 1992.

Labonski, Peter M., and Kunal M. Parker. "Human Rights as Rhetoric: The Persian Gulf War and United States Policy Toward Iraq." *Harvard Human Rights Journal* 4 (1991): 152–162.

Laclau, Ernesto, and Chantal Mouffe. *Hegemony and Socialist Strategy: Towards A Radical Democratic Politics*. Translated by Winston Moore and Paul Cammack. London: Verso, 1985.

LaMarche, Gara. "Managed News, Stifled Views: Free Expression as a Casualty of the Persian Gulf War." *New York Law School Journal of Human Rights* 9 (Fall 1991): 45–83.

Lauterpacht, E., C. J. Greenwood, Marc Weller, and Daniel Bethlehem, eds. *The Kuwait Crisis: Basic Documents*. Cambridge International Documents Series, vol. 1. Cambridge: Grotius Publications, 1991.

Levinas, Emmanuel. *Totality and Infinity*. Translated by Alphonso Lingis. Pittsburgh: Duquesne University Press, 1969.

———. "Ethics as First Philosophy." In *The Levinas Reader,* edited by Sean Hand. Oxford: Basil Blackwell, 1989.

Link, Jurgen. "Fanatics, Fundamentalists, Lunatics, and Drug Traffickers." *Cultural Critique* 19 (Fall 1991): 33–53.

Locke, John. *Two Treatises of Government*. 2d ed. Edited by Peter Laslett. Cambridge: Cambridge University Press, 1967.

Lovins, Amory B., and L. Hunter Lovins. *Making Fuel Efficiency Our Gulf Strategy*. Snowmass: Rocky Mountain Institute, December 1990.

Luban, David. "Just War and Human Rights." *Philosophy and Public Affairs* 9 (Winter 1980): 161–181.

———. "The Romance of the Nation-State." *Philosophy and Public Affairs* 9 (Summer 1980): 239–243.

Luke, Timothy W. "The Discipline of Security Studies and the Codes of Containment: Learning from Kuwait." *Alternatives* 16 (Summer 1991): 315–344.

MacArthur, Brian, ed. *Despatches from the Gulf*. London: Bloomsbury, 1991.

Mariscal, George. "In the Wake of the Gulf War: Untying the Yellow Ribbon." *Cultural Critique* 19 (Fall 1991): 97–117.

Marr, Phebe. *The Modern History of Iraq*. Boulder: Westview, 1985.

McElroy, Robert W. *Morality and American Foreign Policy: The Role of Ethics in International Affairs*. Princeton: Princeton University Press, 1992.

McKinley, Michael. "'The Bitterness of Being Right': Reflections on Australian Alliance Orthodoxy, the Gulf War, and the New World Order." Paper prepared for the annual meeting of the International Studies Association Conference, Atlanta, 31 March–4 April 1992.

Middle East Watch. *Human Rights in Iraq*. New Haven: Yale University Press, 1990.

Nardin, Terry, and David R. Mapel. *Traditions of International Ethics*. Cambridge: Cambridge University Press, 1992.

Norris, Margot. "Military Censorship and the Body Count in the Persian Gulf War." *Cultural Critique* 19 (Fall 1991): 223–245.

Pauker, Guy J. *Military Implications of a Possible World Order Crisis in the 1980s*. A Project AIR FORCE report prepared for the United States Air Force,

R-2003-AF. Santa Monica: The Rand Corporation, November 1977.

Pogge, Thomas. "Liberalism and Global Justice: Hoffmann and Nardin on Morality in International Affairs." *Philosophy and Public Affairs* 15 (Winter 1986): 67–81.

Postol, Theodore A. "Lessons of the Gulf War Experience with Patriot." *International Security* 16 (Winter 1991–1992): 119–171.

Prescott, J. R. V. *Political Frontiers and Boundaries.* London: Allen and Unwin, 1987.

Przybylowicz, Donna, and Abdul JanMohmed. "Introduction: The Economy of Moral Capital in the Gulf War." *Cultural Critique* 19 (Fall 1991): 5–13.

Rajchman, John. *Michel Foucault: The Freedom of Philosophy.* New York: Columbia University Press, 1985.

———. *Truth and Eros.* New York: Routledge, 1991.

"Reflections on the War in the Persian Gulf." *Negotiation Journal* 8 (January 1992): 7–57.

Reich, Robert B. *The Work of Nations: Preparing Ourselves for 21st-Century Capitalism.* New York: Alfred A. Knopf, 1991.

Richelson, Jeffrey T. *The U.S. Intelligence Community.* Cambridge: Ballinger, 1985.

Ridgeway, James, ed. *The March to War.* New York: Four Walls Eight Windows, 1991.

Rosenau, James N., and Ernst-Otto Czempiel. *Governance Without Government: Order and Change in World Politics.* Cambridge: Cambridge University Press, 1992.

Roy, Ramashray, R. B. J. Walker, and Richard K. Ashley. "Dialogue: Towards a Critical Social Theory of International Politics." *Alternatives* 13 (1988): 77–102.

Said, Edward W. *The World, the Text, and the Critic.* Cambridge: Harvard University Press, 1983.

Salinger, Pierre, and Eric Laurent. *Secret Dossier: The Hidden Agenda Behind the Gulf War.* New York: Penguin Books, 1991.

Salemohamed, George. "Levinas: From Ethics to Political Theology." *Economy and Society* 21 (May 1992): 192–206.

Sampson, Anthony. *The Arms Bazaar in the Nineties: From Krupp to Saddam.* London: Coronet Books, 1991.

Schmitt, Carl. *Political Theology.* Cambridge: MIT Press, 1988.

Schofield, Richard. "The Iraq-Kuwait Boundary: A Problem Outstanding." *Middle East International*, 18 April 1991.

Schulte-Sasse, Johan, and Linda Schulte-Sasse. "War, Otherness, and Illusionary Identifications with the State." *Cultural Critique* 19 (Fall 1991): 67–95.

Schurmann, Reiner. *Heidegger on Being and Acting: From Principles to Anarchy.* Bloomington: Indiana University Press, 1987.

Schwarzkopf, Norman, with Peter Petre. *It Doesn't Take a Hero.* New York: Bantam Books, 1992.

Sciolino, Elaine. *The Outlaw State: Saddam Hussein's Quest for Power and the Gulf Crisis.* New York: John Wiley and Sons, 1991.

Scott, Charles E. *The Question of Ethics: Nietzsche, Foucault, Heidegger.* Bloomington: Indiana University Press, 1990.

Shafer, D. Michael. *Deadly Paradigms: The Failure of U.S. Counterinsurgency Policy.* Princeton: Princeton University Press, 1988.

Shapiro, Michael J. "Sovereignty and Exchange in the Orders of Modernity." *Alternatives* 16 (Fall 1991): 447–477.

———. *Reading the Postmodern Polity: Political Theory as Textual Practice.* Minneapolis: University of Minnesota Press, 1992.

Sifry, Micah L., and Christopher Cerf, eds. *The Gulf War Reader: History, Documents, Opinions.* New York: Times Books, 1991.

Simpson, John. *From the House of War.* London: Arrow Books, 1991.

Slotkin, Richard. *Regeneration Through Violence: The Mythology of the American Frontier 1600–1860.* Middletown: Wesleyan University Press, 1973.

Smith, Michael J. *Realist Thought from Weber to Kissinger.* Baton Rouge: Louisiana State University Press, 1986.

Springborg, Robert. "Origins of the Gulf Crisis." *Australian Journal of International Affairs* 44 (December 1990): 221–235.

Staniland, Martin. *Getting to No: The Diplomacy of the Gulf Conflict, August 2, 1990–January 15, 1991.* Pew Case Studies in International Affairs No. 449. Washington, D.C.: Georgetown University, 1992.

Stein, Robert M., and Theodore A. Postol. "Correspondence: Patriot Experience in the Gulf War." *International Security* 17 (Summer 1992): 199–240.

Taylor, Philip M. *War and the Media: Propaganda and Persuasion in the Gulf War.* Manchester: Manchester University Press, 1992.

Tetreault, Mary Ann. "Autonomy, Necessity, and the Small State: Ruling Kuwait in the Twentieth Century." *International Organization* 45 (Autumn 1991): 565–591.

Tiffen, Rodney. "Marching to Whose Drum? Media Battles in the Gulf War." *Australian Journal of International Affairs* 46 (May 1992): 44–60.

Thompson, Kenneth W. *Morality and Foreign Policy.* Baton Rouge: Louisiana State University Press, 1980.

Timmerman, Kenneth R. *The Death Lobby: How the West Armed Iraq.* Boston: Houghton Mifflin, 1991.

Tucker, Robert W., and David C. Hendrickson. *The Imperial Temptation: The New World Order and America's Purpose.* New York: Council on Foreign Relations Press, 1992.

Virilio, Paul. *Speed and Politics: An Essay on Dromology.* Translated by Mark Polizzotti. New York: Semiotext(e), 1986.

Walt, Stephen. "The Renaissance of Security Studies." *International Studies Quarterly* 35 (1991): 211–239.

Walzer, Michael. *Just and Unjust Wars: A Moral Argument with Historical Illustrations.* New York: Basic Books, 1977.

———. "The Moral Standing of States: A Response to Four Critics." *Philosophy and Public Affairs* 9 (Spring 1980): 209–229.

———. "On Just Wars: An Interview with Michael Walzer." *Tikkun* 6 (January 1991).

———. *Just and Unjust Wars: A Moral Argument with Historical Illustrations.* 2d ed. New York: Basic Books, 1992.

Warner, Daniel. *An Ethic of Responsibility in International Relations.* Boulder: Lynne Rienner, 1991.

White, Alan. *Within Nietzsche's Labyrinth.* New York: Routledge, 1991.

White, Hayden. *The Content of the Form: Narrative Discourse and Historical Representation.* Baltimore: The Johns Hopkins University Press, 1987.

White, Stephen. *Political Theory and Postmodernism.* Cambridge: Cambridge University Press, 1991.

Woodward, Bob. *The Commanders.* New York: Simon and Schuster, 1991.

Wyschogrod, Edith. *Saints and Postmodernism: Revisioning Moral Philosophy.*

Chicago: The University of Chicago Press, 1990).
Yant, Martin. *Desert Mirage: The True Story of the Gulf War.* Buffalo: Prometheus Books, 1991.
Young, Marilyn B. "This is Not Vietnam, This is Not a Pipe." *Middle East Report* 171 (July/August 1991): 21–24.

CONGRESSIONAL DOCUMENTS, UN REPORTS, AND U.S. GOVERNMENT REPORTS

Congressional Record. House. 1991–1992. Washington, D.C.
Congressional Research Service. Foreign Affairs and National Defense Division. *Middle East Arms Control and Related Issues.* The Library of Congress, 1991.
United Nations Security Council. *Report to the Secretary General on Humanitarian Needs in Kuwait and Iraq.* S/22366. 1991.
U.S. Congress. House. Committee on Foreign Affairs. *Hearing on Human Rights Abuses in Kuwait and Iraq.* 102nd Cong., 1st sess., 1991.
U.S. Congress. House. Committee on Banking, Finance, and Urban Affairs. *The Role of Banca Nazionale Del Lavoro in Financing Iraq.* 102nd Cong., 1st sess., 1991. Committee Print 102-1.
U.S. Congress. House. Committee on Foreign Affairs. Subcommittee on International Economic Policy and Trade. *Hearing on United States Exports of Sensitive Technology to Iraq.* 102nd Cong., 1st sess., 1991.
U.S. Congress. House. Committee on Banking, Finance, and Urban Affairs. *Hearing on Banca Nazionale Del Lavoro.* 102nd Cong., 1st sess., 1991.
U.S. Congress. House. Committee on Banking, Finance, and Urban Affairs. *Hearing on Iraqi and Banca Nazionale Del Lavoro Participation in Export-Import Programs.* 102nd Cong., 1st sess., 1991.
U.S. Congress. House. Committee on Foreign Affairs. Subcommittee on Arms Control, International Security, and Science. *The Persian Gulf Crisis: Relevant Documents, Correspondence, Reports.* 102nd Cong., 1st sess., 1991. Committee Print 41-288.
U.S. Congress. Senate. Armed Services Committee. *Hearing on FY 93 Defense Budget.* 102nd Cong., 2nd sess., 1992.
U.S. Department of Defense. *Conduct of the Persian Gulf War: Final Report.* 3 vols. Washington, 1992.
Weekly Compilation of Presidential Documents. Washington, 1990.

NEWSPAPERS, MAGAZINES, AND TELEVISION PROGRAMS

ABC News, *Nightline,* 1991–1992.
Atlantic Monthly, 1991.
Boston Globe, 1992.
CBS News, *60 Minutes,* 1992.
Facts on File, 1990.
Financial Times (London), 1990–1992.
The Independent (London), 1990–1991.
Los Angeles Times, 1990–1992.
Manchester Guardian Weekly, 1990–1992.

Mother Jones, 1991.
The Nation, 1990–1992.
NBC News, *Dateline NBC*, 1992.
New Perspectives Quarterly, 1992.
New Republic, 1991–1992.
Newsweek, 1992.
The New Yorker, 1990–1991.
New York Review of Books, 1992.
New York Times, 1990–1992.
The Observer (London), 1990.
The Progressive, 1991.
St. Petersburg Times (Florida), 1991.
Village Voice, 1991.
Wall Street Journal, 1991–1992.
Washington Post, 1990–1992.

Index

113

About the Book
and the Author

Unlike other analyses of the Gulf War, this book examines the discursive practices and political strategies that obscured the issues involved in the Gulf region and moved the crisis toward conflict. In particular, Campbell probes the discourse of moral certitude through which the United States and its allies located with Iraq—in unambiguous ethical terms—the responsibility for evil.

Seeking neither to exculpate one side nor condemn the other, Campbell offers an alternative narrative of the Gulf conflict. His discussions of Kuwait's border, Iraq's relations with the West, the complex nature of the grievances behind the conflict and the possibilities for their nonmilitary resolution, the moral turpitude of the participants, and the conduct of the war all serve to challenge the way IR theory has conventionally understood the questions of agency, power, ethics, responsibility, and sovereignty.

The book concludes with an outline of how a formulation of ethics attuned to the radically interdependent character of world politics would refigure theories of international relations and the practice of foreign policy.

DAVID CAMPBELL is assistant professor of political science at the Johns Hopkins University. His publications include *Writing Security: U.S. Foreign Policy and the Politics of Identity.*

Other Books in the Series

Trancending the State-Global Divide: The Neostructural Agenda in International Relations
    Ronen Palan and Barry Gills, editors
The Global Economy as Political Space
    Stephan J. Rosow, Naeen Inayatullah, and Mark Rupert, editors
The Discourses of World Politics: A Critical Introduction to International Relations
    Jim George